Did Saint Paul Deviate From The Gospel?

notionpress
.com

Did Saint Paul Deviate From The Gospel?

Devapraksh R. Shampur

notionpress
.com

Notion Press

5 Muthu Kalathy Street, Triplicane,

Chennai - 600 005

First Published by Notion Press 2014

ISBN: 978-93-84878-11-5

"And ye shall know the truth, and the truth shall make you free" (John 8:32).

This book is dedicated to all those who thirst to know the truth (Matthew 5:6).

"These were more noble than those in Thessalonica, in that they received the word with all readiness of mind, and searched the scriptures daily, whether those things were so" (Acts 17:11).

CONTENTS

INTRODUCTION

Christianity became a religion when it started giving undue importance to Paul's writings right from the beginning over others and other writings including the preaching of Jesus found in the four books of the Gospel! Paul—a rank outsider—has practically replaced Jesus in thinking and observance! Jesus never came to establish a new religion but came to take us to higher spiritual realm of understanding of the Scripture and make that to help us lead a transformed life.

For those who are seeking eternal life in heaven, not goodies of this world, it is important to go back to the roots or base, that is, the Gospel that gives information to enhance the knowledge of our Saviour who is the truth. All writings are to be held against this brilliant light, that is, truth for our spiritual growth. Otherwise, we may be bogged down by religious rituals to our own destruction! This book is a sincere attempt to draw attention to the words of truth as spoken by Jesus and propounded by His first chosen apostles. In this attempt, the reader is urged to ignore writings and verses that do not complement the Gospel nor supported by other writings. There cannot be a monopoly of the truth! All important concepts and theology cannot be formed on the basis of one single verse, on one author or book. Truth should be viewed from different directions to arrive at its absolute value. That is the reason God with His infinite wisdom gave us four books of the Gospel to understand His

Son! What is expected of the readers is to approach this with no preconceived notions and uphold all that glorifies Jesus Christ whether it is of Paul or others!

Right from my young age, I have always sought to know God, His attributes and the truth. Apart from visiting various pilgrimage centres, I was a voracious reader of all kinds of literary books. Having my own juvenile lust and later as an young man still under the spell of fleshly weaknesses, my reading ranged from pornographic to philosophical works!

In the course of time, I read Mahatma Gandhi's autography "My Experiments With Truth" in which he said that his life was very much influenced by three books, namely, "Sermon on the Mount" recorded in the Bible, "The Kingdom of God is Within you" by Leo Tolstoy and "Unto This Last" by John Ruskin. Even though Gandhi remained a Hindu, he was charged of having a Christian heart! Using the essence of the preaching of Jesus Christ, he brought to the knees the mighty Christian world of the British Empire! Of course, further readings eventually made me to accept Jesus Christ as my Saviour eventually. However, Gandhi who had read the Bible had indicated that St. Paul, who was a learned scholar, distorted the Gospel! Even after I became a Christian, this remark of Gandhi bothered me a lot. I read several versions of the Bible including Kannada version that is in my mother tongue. Extensive discussions in various Christian Forums comprising of members from all over the world followed by detailed Bible studies and fellowships, spanning nearly four decades, eventually led me to believe, after all, Gandhi was right!

It is not that I want to write off Paul altogether; he suffered a lot and took great pains to spread the Gospel to the

Gentiles, but he clearly overstepped his limits my dominating the semi-literate apostles who were called specifically by Jesus in His earthly ministry! He did write great amount to encourage new believers, but, at the same time, being not aware of the entire preaching and life of Jesus, he assumed certain things that deviated from the sublime and profound teaching of Jesus! Therefore, it is necessary to find out what can be accepted of Paul and what to ignore of his writings. In essence we need to apply the four books of the Gospel that are available to us now completed—which were not during Paul's ministry—to the writings of Paul to filter out verses of his that contradict the message of Jesus. This is exactly my endeavour in writing this book. I solicit the reader of this book to apply his mind without any preconceived bias to know the truth, nothing but the truth, to the extent that is possible with the help of the Holy Spirit. We shall bear in mind that salvation depends on following Jesus, not anyone else with their own understanding that includes Paul too! No one should come between Jesus and us, no matter what whether it is Paul or Peter or Mary, or even any saints or any preacher under any pretext!

1

Paul's Apostleship

Paul appears to stumble right from the start when it comes to understanding the preaching of Jesus since he was not a part of the earthly ministry of Jesus! Whatever preaching Jesus made was conveyed to him by Peter—to what extent we cannot be sure—when he stayed with Peter after his conversion. This is seen in his letter to Galatians: "Then after three years I went up to Jerusalem to see Peter, and abode with him fifteen days" (Galatians 1:18).

Paul started claiming the apostleship without understanding the spiritual significance of the number 12 that Jesus used to choose 12 apostles to begin with for His ministry on earth. The number 12 represented the twelve tribes related to Jacob. The 12 apostles meant to judge them as Jesus declared, "Verily I say unto you, that ye which have followed me, in the regeneration when the Son of man shall sit in the throne of his glory, ye also shall sit upon twelve thrones, judging the twelve tribes of Israel" (Matthew 19:28).

Therefore, there was no question of Paul becoming a 13th apostle unless he had plans to have his own tribe extra which was unlikely since he remained single!

Also Peter clearly defined who should be selected as an apostle after Judas Iscariot committed suicide. He said, "For it is written in the book of Psalms, let his habitation be desolate, and let no man dwell therein: and his bishoprick let another take. Wherefore of these men which have companied with us all the time that the Lord Jesus went in and out among us, beginning from the baptism of John, unto that same day that he was taken up from us, must one be ordained to be a witness with us of his resurrection."

And they appointed two, Joseph called Barsabas, who was surnamed Justus, and Matthias.

And they prayed, and said, Thou, Lord, which knowest the hearts of all *men,* shew whether of these two thou hast chosen, that he may take part of this ministry and apostleship, from which Judas by transgression fell, that he might go to his own place. And they gave forth their lots; and the lot fell upon Matthias; and he was numbered with the eleven apostles (Acts 1:20-26).

Many 'pick-and-choose' Pauline Christians do not want to accept this replacement of Matthias for Judas Iscariot by Peter only because they want to rebut the succession claim of spiritual authority from Peter by Roman Catholic Popes!

They tend to argue that Peter acted without the guidance of the Holy Spirit because the Holy Spirit was given first during the Pentecost. It only proves that they are ignorant of the blessing of Jesus on the ten apostles breathing them the Holy Spirit after His resurrection as can be seen from this verse: "And when he had said this, he breathed on them, and saith unto them, receive ye the Holy Ghost" (John 20:22). Peter wanted the group to be completed with 12 persons in the absence of Judas, who betrayed Jesus, before starting on any work related to sharing of the Gospel and baptizing the new believers!

Paul did not qualify any of the conditions the great apostle Peter stipulated before choosing Mathias! James who took up the leadership of Jerusalem Church did not claim to be an apostle in his letter even though Paul and Luke appear to consider him to be an apostle! Obviously, both missed out the spiritual significance of the number 12. Same thing holds good in case of Jude. Even as secular half-brother, he did not claim apostleship in his letter.

In contrast, Paul repeatedly self-claimed himself to be an apostle going by the common understanding of the word in a secular world! Both Luke and Paul, the rank outsiders, tend to call some others also as apostles against the spirit behind in calling of 12 apostles by Jesus!

From the following verse one can see that Luke who wrote the book of Acts considered Barnabas and Paul as apostles too:

"Which when the apostles, Barnabas and Paul, heard of, they rent their clothes, and ran in among the people, crying out" (Acts 14:14); and Paul considered James as an apostle along with him: "But other of the apostles saw I none, save James the Lord's brother" (Galatians 1:19).

However, the apostle John who was dear to Jesus made clear cut clarification after Paul had created confusion in apostleship by his later book of Revelation:

"I know thy works, and thy labour, and thy patience, and how thou canst not bear them which are evil: and thou hast tried them which say they are apostles, and are not, and hast found them liars" (Revelation 2:2).

It is further endorsed by the following verse that fixes the number 12, no more, no less!

"And the wall of the city had twelve foundations, and in them the names of the twelve apostles of the Lamb" (Revelation 21:14).

The problem that Paul had was that he wanted the authority of apostleship because he did not get proper reception and hearing to his preaching about Jesus Christ when he was preaching in Arabia immediately after conversion and later after meeting the apostles through Barnabas. Nothing has been recorded of his preaching during that period.

But only when Paul got the support of the apostles in Jerusalem and accompanied Barnabas in his first missionary journey along with Mark, he was able to realize the encouraging results! Without this support, probably, Paul's work would have become any other missionary work of repute mentionable at best or totally forgotten and unrecorded at worst! It would not have brought him the importance he generated with this support and recognition, leading to complete domination in the Christendom right from the beginning!

Paul with his Pharisaic background and scholarship mixed with shrewdness sensed his superiority in knowledge in the OT writings compared to semi-literate and gentle minded Barnabas and Mark in their first mission work. Consequently, he sets his own terms for second missionary journey, unbecoming of a Christian!

Probably, Mark might have sensed Paul's domineering spirit during their mission, and that might have resulted in Mark deciding to quit the mission when half way through. However, Barnabas, with his humility of giving Mark another chance as any believing Christian would do, was opposed by Paul, who never knew compassionate and forgiving Jesus personally well, and, consequently, he initiates the first division in the Jerusalem Church.

"And Barnabas determined to take with them John, whose surname was Mark," and "and the contention was so sharp between them, that they departed asunder one from the other: and so Barnabas took Mark, and sailed unto Cyprus" (Acts 15:37, 39).

Unfortunately, this has set a trend in all Paul believing groups creating divisions after divisions! Basically, it has become a practice of picking a verse from Paul and parting ways!

Of course, the self-claim of apostleship was questioned during his ministry. For that reason, he kept on driving home his claim forcibly time and again that can be seen by a couple of these verses:

"Am I not an apostle? Am I not free? Have I not seen Jesus Christ our Lord? Are not ye my work in the Lord?" and "if I be not an apostle unto others, yet doubtless I am to you: for the seal of mine apostleship are ye in the Lord" (1 Corinthians 9:1&2).

These claims of apostleship abound in his letters written away from the place to which they were addressed to. We do not know what type of answers he gave when he was questioned when he was available in person! The examples are:

"Have we not power to lead about a sister, a wife, as well as other apostles, and as the brethren of the Lord, and Cephas?" (1 Corinthians 9:5); "for I speak to you Gentiles, inasmuch as I am the apostle of the Gentiles, I magnify mine office" (Romans 11:13); and "(For he that wrought effectually in Peter to the apostleship of the circumcision, the same was mighty in me toward the Gentiles)" (Galatians 2:8).

Jesus called Paul a 'chosen vessel' never an apostle. So, unfortunately, Paul without proper understanding of Jesus of His call wanted apostleship! Furthermore, Jesus never separately called Peter an apostle for the circumcision and Paul an apostle of the Gentiles!

Jesus commanded Paul this way: "But the Lord said unto him, go thy way: for he is a chosen vessel unto me, to bear my name before the Gentiles, and kings, and the children of Israel" (Acts 9:15).

Both Peter and Paul were called to witness for both the Jews and Gentiles. Both witnessed to both the groups initially. Paul, when he encountered stiff opposition to his ministry, decided to take an easy path of confining to Gentiles with whom he can manage easily on his own—against the directive of Jesus—since they did not know much of One true God and the Law of God. This was recorded by Luke as follows:

"Then Paul and Barnabas waxed bold, and said, It was necessary that the word of God should first have been spoken to you: but seeing ye put it from you, and judge yourselves unworthy of everlasting life, lo, we turn to the Gentiles" (Acts 13:46).

Paul was also boasting of signs and miracles through him as a sign of apostleship as he wrote to Corinthians: "Truly the signs of an apostle were wrought among you in all patience, in signs, and wonders, and mighty deeds" (2 Corinthians12:12).

That was not a big thing! Such signs and authority were given to other disciples also before. No one claimed apostleship because of that! Furthermore, Jesus cautioned that anti-Christ people will also perform such deeds and indicated that what was important was fruit of the Spirit in a man and lawful behaviour as can be seen from the following verses:

"Every tree that bringeth not forth good fruit is hewn down, and cast into the fire.

Wherefore by their fruits ye shall know them. Not every one that saith unto me, Lord, Lord, shall enter into the kingdom of heaven; but he that doeth the will of my Father which is in heaven.

Many will say to me in that day, Lord, Lord, have we not prophesied in thy name? And in thy name have cast out devils? And in thy name done many wonderful works? And then will I profess unto them, I never knew you: depart from me, ye that work iniquity" (Matthew 7:19 to 23).

Jesus went further to give warning as follows:

"For many shall come in my name, saying, I am Christ; and shall deceive many"; "Then if any man shall say unto you, Lo, here is Christ, or there; believe it not" and "For there shall arise false Christs, and false prophets, and shall shew great signs and wonders; insomuch that, if it were possible, they shall deceive the very elect" (Matthew 24:5, 23, 24).

In brief, one can say that Paul never knew the preaching of Jesus fully well and the spiritual symbolism of the number twelve! Consequently, he, perhaps, unknowingly usurped the authority and status of an apostle! As a result, many modern day evangelists and workers also make a self-claim of being apostles as a part of their livelihood mocking at the wisdom of the Lord in choosing His first twelve apostles amongst many of His disciples:

"And when it was day, he called *unto him* his disciples: and of them he chose twelve, whom also he named apostles" (Luke 6:13).

2
Misleading Communion

It was the great dedicated and devoted work of saints and clergy of Roman Catholics that preserved many writings of apostles and disciples. They also diligently made several copies for all to refer in their service of sharing the Gospel. Without them and their work there was no question of Protestants claiming the authority of the writings! However, Catholics give more importance to the traditions, rituals and defined sacraments! We do not find much quoting of verses from Paul's epistles in their decrees and subsequent writings of their saints. Whereas almost all theological discussions of Protestants are based very much on Paul's writings! Paul's epistles might not have dominated in the thinking of Catholics, but, certainly, he has left a permanent dominance in the ritual of communion that was instituted by him alone!

Paul being crafty, as admitted by him, (2 Corinthians 12:16: "But be it so, I did not burden you: nevertheless, being crafty, I caught you with guile"), he came up with a solution for the disorderly behaviour in the notorious Corinthian church with an introduction of this ritual much against the words of the Lord! Let us read what Paul wrote in this regard:

"For I have received of the Lord that which also I delivered unto you, that the Lord Jesus the *same* night in which he was betrayed took bread: And when he had given thanks, he brake *it,* and said, 'Take, eat: this is my body, which is broken for you: this do in remembrance of me.' After the same manner also *he took* the cup, when he had supped, saying, 'this cup is the new testament in my blood: this do ye, as oft as ye drink *it*, in remembrance of me.' For as often as ye eat this bread, and drink *this* cup, ye do shew the Lord's death till he come" (1 Corinthians 11: 23 to 26).

You see here clearly Paul telling a 'white lie' that the Lord had asked the apostles to repeat the Lord's last supper as a token of 'remembrance' of His death! Nothing can be achieved by glorifying the death of any person for that matter! Particularly, in the case of the Lord, it is His resurrection that needs to be proclaimed boldly! Paul was not a witness to the Last Supper. Mathew who was there never mentioned about 'remembering' in his book of the Gospel. This was what he recorded:

"And as they were eating, Jesus took bread, and blessed *it*, and brake *it*, and gave *it* to the disciples, and said, 'Take, eat; this is my body.' And he took the cup, and gave thanks, and gave *it* to them, saying, 'Drink ye all of it; for this is my blood of the new testament, which is shed for many for the remission of sins. But I say unto you, I will not drink henceforth of this fruit of the vine, until that day when I drink it new with you in my Father's kingdom' " (Matthew 26: 26 to 29).

Not only the Lord never mentioned about repeating this as a 'remembrance' act, but also said that He will never drink fruit of the vine until the day in Father's kingdom.

What about John who was there at that time. He also never mentions about observing this ritual as a 'remembrance' of the Lord's death. Instead he elaborated on the significance of this observance that should be made clear to all those who accept Jesus as their Lord and Saviour with the following supporting verses:

"Then Jesus said unto them, 'Verily, verily, I say unto you, except ye eat the flesh of the Son of man, and drink his blood, ye have no life in you. Whoso eateth my flesh, and drinketh my blood, hath eternal life; and I will raise him up at the last day. For my flesh is meat indeed, and my blood is drink indeed. He that eateth my flesh, and drinketh my blood, dwelleth in me, and I in him' " (John 6:53 to 56).

If we referred to other writings considered as a part of apocryphal, you will find apostles breaking the bread signifying this acceptance symbolically and observed more or less immediately after baptism.

Breaking of bread indicated in the book of Acts on some occasions also informed of common communal meal on the first day of a week that was observed in Jerusalem Church with believers. As new believers were added daily in Jerusalem after the Pentecost, breaking of bread and drinking the vine was also observed symbolically in tune with the above verses of John practically every week.

We read as follows:

"And they continued stedfastly in the apostles' doctrine and fellowship, and in breaking of bread, and in prayers. And fear came upon every soul: and many wonders and signs were done by the apostles. And all that believed were together, and had all things common; and sold their possessions and goods, and parted them to all *men,* as every man had need. And they, continuing daily with one accord in the temple, and breaking bread from house to house, did eat their meat with gladness and singleness of heart, praising God, and having favour with all the people. And the Lord added to the church daily such as should be saved" (Acts 2: 42 to 47).

So we can see that both communal meal and communion being observed with new believers. Communion was not meant as a ritual to be observed with a regular frequency in the absence of newly baptized members. Communion was meant as a celebration of winning souls as directed by Jesus. It was not meant as a ritual with all old believers frequently!

Therefore, the ritual of communion was not established by the Lord during the Last Supper to be observed frequently to commemorate His death. The Gospel of Mark did not mention that ritual has to be observed as a token of 'remembrance'. Gospel of Mark was basically written on behalf of Peter by Mark. Of course, Peter was a partaker during the Last Supper.

What about Luke. He was not a party in the Last Supper. This is what we see in his book of the Gospel:

"For I say unto you, 'I will not any more eat thereof, until it be fulfilled in the kingdom of God.' And he took the cup, and gave thanks, and said, 'Take this, and divide *it* among yourselves: For I say unto you, I will not drink of the fruit of the vine, until the kingdom of God shall come.' And he took bread, and gave thanks, and brake *it,* and gave unto them, saying, 'This is my body which is given for you: this do in remembrance of me' (v.19). Likewise also the cup after supper, saying, 'This cup *is* the new testament in my blood, which is shed for you' (v.20)" (Luke 22:16 to 20).

Here also the Lord said that He will not eat and drink further until everything is fulfilled in the kingdom of God. Only in the verse 19, we find the word 'remembrance' mentioned. However, further research indicates that verses 19 and 20 were later insertions and not found in some ancient manuscripts! Additions may be the short work of biased Paul's people later to support Paul's verses in 1 Corinthians that have been indicated earlier! 1 Corinthians was written earlier to Luke's Gospel so also other three books.

What was instituted on the day of Last Supper was the new covenant (testament) in blood as indicated in the verse 20 above, so also in Matthew 26:28, not communion as a ritual that needed to be observed at any desired frequency with same people over and over again! It will be meaningful if observed whenever new believers are added. That pleases God too: "Likewise, I say unto you, 'there is joy in the presence of the angels of God over one sinner that repenteth'" (Luke 15:10).

It is interesting to note that all kinds of different frequencies are observed by Christendom. Unfortunately, what is forgotten is the fact that Jesus fulfilled the Law and brought an end to all kinds of rituals that associated with the OT dictum. His Last Supper also happened to be last Passover for His believers. It was no longer an annual ritual or of any frequency, but of observance of seeking His communion through His words of preaching. Those who prayerfully study His words (Bread) anytime are actually observing the communion, and that should lead to a holy life (blood) with proper understanding. That is precisely, spiritually speaking, eating the bread of life and drinking of fruit of vine that lead to eternal life!

Hence, when the spirit behind the communion is not observed, one can expect all kinds of bizarre concepts and thinking based on the ritual of communion established by Paul.

Salvation Army denomination does not observe this at all at any time. Jehovah Witnesses observe this once in a year with a hint to many not to eat elements offered to them because they believe that those who partake in the elements are spurred by the spirit and will be one amongst 12000 groups indicated in the book of Revelation! Brethren Assemblies observe every week so also Catholics. Many other denominations observe once in a month along with regular Sunday service separately in the morning for convenience! Some observe in the evenings specially gathered for this purpose with teaching also. Catholics believe that the elements turn into the body and blood of Jesus mysteriously during this observance!

Brethren Assemblies have this observed at the beginning of their worship services. Many walk out after this formality ignoring the sharing of the word which is more important, and it is the one that spiritually denotes the communion and life, not mere breaking of bread! Many denominations insist on single loaf of bread and a glass of wine for sharing. Actually unleavened bread was used during Passover of the OT times and when Jesus had His Last Supper. In other places pieces of bread and several small cups of grape juice will be served to the believers where they are seated. At other places, believers kneel before the altar and get compressed piece of bread and grape juice in a small cup individually administered by a pastor. Puritans had objected to kneeling for the elements earlier several centuries ago.

What is that we can conclude from all these divergent procedure? Jesus gave the Great Commission of making disciples and baptizing them along with teaching what He had commanded the apostles during His ministry. There are three things involved in His directive, namely, reaching out, baptizing and teaching what He had said. Unfortunately, the first two is taken care of whereas the last one is ignored because it cannot be easily practiced! So the easy way out was to pick the easiest thing of participating in the formality of communion ignoring the spiritual understanding of the same as indicated in the Gospel of John quoted earlier.

Therefore, the spiritless formality of observing the communion came into the fore very soon in the early history of the churches. This was further encouraged by Paul with a 'white lie' of using the word 'remembrance' in one of his early letters when the Gospel was not fully available in written form!

Therefore, I need to reiterate that unless Paul's thinking is supported by other books of the Bible in the NT, it is better to ignore such instructions from him. They were not meant for us but only applicable to people of that place and situation with that special problem for that time--being given room for spiritual growth in subsequent days, months or years!

Spiritual growth is not an instantaneous phenomenon! Apostles made mistakes and grew gradually in their faith and knowledge of the Saviour leaving behind their old selves, so also Paul. Paul with his previous pharisaic background and religious bent of mind offered solutions to ill reputed Corinthian church that led to religious ritual of communion! Jesus never planned on a new religion; His method was fulfilment of the ceremonial laws leading to a higher spiritual growth in thoughts and deeds. But there is always a tendency to revert back to easy religion and rituals with man-made doctrines.

Hence, a meticulous study of the scriptures clearly indicates that it was a ritual instituted by Paul to tackle the problem in notorious Corinthian Church established by him!

What is not difficult to follow: ritual of communion or abiding by the blood Covenant that is the law of Christ?

Obviously, it is the communion procedure. People, naturally, settle for convenient arrangements avoiding the harder aspects, giving unnecessary importance and branding for an easy observance! Jesus never wanted this to be observed as a routine ritual!

Even Paul did not fix up a frequency for this, like, daily, weekly, monthly or yearly observance! Paul was never with Jesus in His earthly ministry, so he missed out many important tenets preached by Jesus! All the apostles grew in spiritual stature gradually. Paul still had his pharisaic mind in the beginning! He simply came up with a solution at Corinth with a ritual, influenced by his old nature with an eagerness to solve the problem based on the reports he had received!

That was not the case with the apostles. If you happened to go through the apocryphal books, such as, Acts according to Peter and Thomas, you will find that they observed the spirit of communion based on what Jesus Christ preached: "Truly, truly, I say to you, unless you eat the flesh of the Son of Man and drink His blood, you have no life in yourselves. He who eats My flesh and drinks My blood has eternal life, and I will raise him up on the last day. For My flesh is true food, and My blood is true drink. He who eats My flesh and drinks My blood abides in Me, and I in him" (John 6:53-56).

The new believers who accepted Him as their Saviour should also believe in what He said symbolically with a spiritual sense. The communion was observed in the early Churches—that directly involved apostles—with new believers understanding the spirit behind what the Lord had said.

What is spiritual cannot be converted to a routine practice! The communion will be meaningful only, as I have indicated before, when it is celebrated with new believers immediately after baptism. That also gives credence to the 'Great Commission' advocated by the Lord as a part of the responsibility of a believer. Heaven will rejoice when a new believer is brought before the Lord! What other occasions other than communion is fit to solemnize this event with the angels and other believers?

What is happening now in Churches? All kinds of bizarre thinking and belief go with that! Thinking that Jesus Christ will become body and blood in the elements of bread and wine is not supported by the Bible! Such an uncalled for belief will make everyone a kind of a cannibal! Not only that, it is a sadistic thinking of expecting Jesus Christ to get crucified and shed blood whenever communion is observed!

In the book of Acts breaking of the bread may signify both communal meal and communion or just one of the two. This performance was recorded several times since new batches of believers were added in succession in Jerusalem after the Pentecost.

Communion was never observed before the Pentecost. Why did they not observe before if it had been indicated during the Last Supper? Its first observance was recorded after 3000 people were baptized: "Then they that gladly received his word were baptized: and the same day there were added *unto them* about three thousand souls. And they continued stedfastly in the apostles' doctrine and fellowship, and in breaking of bread, and in prayers" (Acts 2:41 & 42).

Communion has nothing to do with our salvation, that too, when it is being carried out as a ritual! Many churches give too much of importance to this part of service relegating the word of God! In some churches people come only for this and walk away immediately afterwards without sharing the word, and in some others where word is shared first and communion taken later, people join for latter later! What is important: inspired words of the God or the elements of the communion? It is a typical tendency of people going after created elements rather than hearing the words of the Creator!

Now churches excommunicate people who do not go by its doctrines and its governance. They are prevented from participating in the communion! A big deal! Who can prevent a person in hearing the word of God?

In some other churches, one has to compulsorily participate for certain number of times in a year to claim a right to exercise his franchise in church elections! These people are after secular power and rights down on earth, and they do not want to set their minds on things spiritual up in heaven!

These different beliefs, procedures and practices clearly prove that the entire communion concept is a man-made doctrine, and it is not one single truth! Meaningless rituals ended with spiritual teaching of Jesus. Of course, it is worthwhile to mention here that baptism is not a ritual for an individual! Immersion water baptism is done once for a believing person in the name of the Father, the Son and the Holy Spirit. Insistence of re-baptism for joining another denomination is a big sham!

3

The Worst Relapse: Speaking in Tongues

Protestantism reached a very low level in spirituality in Pentecostal movement that started in USA about one hundred years back! Naturally, people with emotional bent of mind started behaving without self-control (fruit of the Spirit)—a dangerous trend of grieving the Holy Spirit—and claimed it as the work of the Holy Spirit! It was the spirit of the person which was behaving and exhibiting animal instincts of speaking gibberish even though, we know, God has bestowed humankind the art of logical speech and articulations!

Actually 'Pentecostal movement' was a misnomer; it is the worst relapse of the notorious Corinthian church's condition. The U.S.A. with its badly fermented society of liberalism, permissiveness, promiscuity and indulgence gave birth to a condition that was similar to Corinth about 2000 years ago.

These people started behaving, when once inside a church, as if God had become deaf and blind and that required shouting and acrobatics to draw His attention! With their delusion they replaced God the Father with the Son with their whacky theology! Now all kinds of people, homosexuals, lesbians, women pastors, divorced, abortionists, feminists et al can claim spiritual authority by out of control gestures and shouts!

What about the miracles of healing that were and are being observed with this movement? Only wicked generation seeks signs as pointed out by Jesus: "A wicked and adulterous generation seeketh after a sign; and there shall no sign be given unto it, but the sign of the prophet Jonas. And he left them, and departed" (Matthew 16:4).

People will always be looking for profitable things of the present life rather on a permanent life of eternal value! When Jesus fed them with food, they wanted to make him a king! ("When Jesus therefore perceived that they would come and take him by force, to make him a king, he departed again into a mountain himself alone"-- John 6:15).

Both the healer and the healed may lose salvation if they did not produce the fruit of the Spirit! Miracles of healing are being observed in other religions, other sects and denominations of Christendom. They are also being accomplished by sorcerers through black magic and with the control of evil spirits! Jesus also warned that anti-Christ will perform greater miracles than what they might have observed.

What is important is the means employed to effect miracles. If behaviour that go with that performance disgrace or mock at the Lord, then such acts should be shunned. No matter what type of dreaded disease I might have, I will not approach a person who talks gibberish and misbehaves to get cured. I am seeking eternal life, not just physical well being for a short duration of life on earth through any kind of witchcraft or misbehaviour!

Pentecostal movement is spreading like wild fire with their wild behaviour! That is because people are prone to incline towards base animal instincts. They are least interested in developing spiritual traits!

Jesus warned, "Enter ye in at the strait gate: for wide *is* the gate, and broad *is* the way, that leadeth to destruction, and many there be which go in thereat. Because strait *is* the gate, and narrow *is* the way, which leadeth unto life, and few there be that find it. Beware of false prophets, which come to you in sheep's clothing, but inwardly they are ravening wolves. Ye shall know them by their fruits. Do men gather grapes of thorns, or figs of thistles? Even so every good tree bringeth forth good fruit; but a corrupt tree bringeth forth evil fruit. A good tree cannot bring forth evil fruit, neither *can* a corrupt tree bring forth good fruit. Every tree that bringeth not forth good fruit is hewn down, and cast into the fire. Wherefore by their fruits ye shall know them" (Matthew 7:13 to 20).

Instead of developing the fruit of the Spirit of self-control, they are giving undue importance to spiritual gifts like merchants of a trade!

This movement was based on what Paul wrote to a notorious Church in Corinth based on the reports he had received on a phenomenon called 'speaking in tongue'. Paul, as usual, came up with a claim that he also spoke many tongues! Fortunately, he did not do that inside a church! Perhaps, he had received letters for and against this happening! He came up with a solution, sitting elsewhere, by introducing a concept of having an interpreter!

Nowhere in the Bible, except in Corinthians, have we noticed the requirement of an interpreter! That is because the speaking in tongue was observed for the first time on Pentecost. At that event, the Holy Spirit spoke through people in many different existing foreign languages that were understood by a few people present there. No interpretation was done! Throughout the book of Acts similar utterances were heard that required no interpreter. That means the Holy Spirit spoke on all those occasions in a foreign language unknown to the person speaking but recognized by a few present there. It was marvellous to witness the awesome power of the Holy Spirit!

But what was happening in Corinth was that emotionally charged people were speaking gibberish motivated by their personal (human) spirits! It was not the Holy Spirit speaking through persons. They called this gibberish talk (unintelligent talk) as an unknown language! This, Paul thought, required an interpreter!

In the following two verses, notice the use of plural word 'spirits' is indicating the spirits of the people involved. It is nothing to do with the involvement of the Holy Spirit because there is only one Holy Spirit.

"And to another the effecting of miracles, and to another prophecy, and to another the distinguishing of spirits, to another various kinds of tongues, and to another the interpretation of tongues" (I Corinthians 12:10).

"And the spirits of prophets are subject to prophets" (I Corinthians 14:32).

Speaking in tongue may be claimed as a spiritual gift, but it is least desired! Paul urges people to seek superior gifts. Once the gift is given the giver has nothing to do with it! It is like receiving a gift of a kitchen knife. It can be used for cutting vegetables or killing someone! Subsequently, the believers heeded to the advice of Paul, and this ungainly phenomenon stopped in churches.

Like people who seek a kind of satisfaction and pleasure in drugs, deluded Christians have taken refuge in this method to get a feeling of relief in venting out their uncontrolled emotions and animal instincts inside a church! This they claim to be the work of the Holy Spirit! No way, they can drag the Holy Spirit to their low level of indulgence!

Very amusing thing in some of the Pentecostal churches is that the congregation will be shouting, howling and making animal noises along with physically degrading activities of rolling over the floor, jumping up and down, etc., but when a pastor raises his hand to stop this nuisance, they stop and remain quiet! If they had been acting like this motivated by the Holy Spirit, a pastor will have no authority to ask the Holy Spirit to stop!

What is happening in many Pentecostal churches is best understood by the following verse:

"But the Spirit explicitly says that in later times some will fall away from the faith, paying attention to deceitful spirits and doctrines of demons" (I Timothy 4:1).

One German believer had this to say: when she was in USA on a visit, she visited a nearby Pentecostal church. She noticed that many were speaking gibberish which was not understood by the English congregation. Shockingly, she noticed that they were cursing God in German; that was what she clearly heard! She simply rushed out of the church!

As I have been maintaining from the beginning, Pentecostal people also do have some merits in their beliefs and practices! But demerits overrule the merits exceedingly, warranting us to avoid their fellowship inside their churches and disregard their unspiritual claims of authority in their doctrines! Therefore Paul's cautioning Timothy in the above mentioned verse is in the right spirit!

Why should God require an interpreter in addition to one who is uttering to make known His thoughts?

Salvation and fellowship are directly related to God with no interference or intervention by another! The Holy Spirit would never consider such an option of interpretation when He can directly interact with a believer to inspire, motivate or speak up!

"But when they deliver you up, take no thought how or what ye shall speak: for it shall be given you in that same hour what ye shall speak. For it is not ye that speak, but the Spirit of your Father which speaketh in you" (Matthew 10:19, 20).

Paul also says that when there is no interpreter, one should keep quiet! As indicated before, nobody can ask the Holy Spirit to keep quiet when He is speaking through another person! It was never done anywhere else. Obviously this speaking gibberish and interpretation has nothing to do with the cause of the Holy Spirit, but just emotional outbursts of persons applicable to both the speaker and interpreter! There is no convincing proof that an interpreter is translating correctly what is spoken in gibberish by another person! We need to test the spirits.

These groups who speak gibberish are claiming falsely that they are filled with the Spirit! What an absurd and intoxicated claim! These people love to go to church to release their emotional instincts since exhibiting such an activity outside brands them as mental misfits! Outside their churches they are as good or as bad as other nominal Christians! Their spiritual life ends after they come out of the church to start a typical life of uttering lies, irresponsibility, etc., since they will have enjoyed to the brim their oral and physical ebullition for a couple of hours that was reserved for Sunday aggregated in a period of six days! Since they think they are blessed by the Holy Spirit on Sundays inside a church, they hardly understand and lead a life of honesty and integrity after they come out!

Without an honest revival of the Gospel and its message, I believe that misguided Christians face a bleak future! To borrow from saying of a person who had suffered: 'God cannot be confused with life'! Worldly life is not a measure of heavenly blessings! 'Prosperity-gospel' groups are the by-products of this ugly cultist movement! All our actions and motives should be based on what is revealed in the Bible endorsed by many sources, not just one epistle.

Paul stayed in Corinth for nearly one and a half years. Question is why he was forced to write so many behavioural and spiritual corrections using his pragmatism after receiving letters seeking his advice? It appears people started mocking at what happened at Pentecost with what they might have heard from others after Paul left! Reading through the letters of Paul is like listening to one side of a telephone conversation without being aware of what actually was happening and spoken from the other side! Now after more than 2000 years, people are making a 'mountain out of a mole hill'! Many have come up with a strange theory that adhering to 1 Corinthian epistle is a full Gospel worship! Nothing is farther than this from the truth! Their naive thinking makes them to accept all kinds of logic.

For example, they think when a person speaks gibberish (unknown tongue) immediately after baptism, it is taken as a known foreign language—existing in some corner of the world—unknown to the baptized. It also remains unrecognized by the persons present there. They do not expect that to be interpreted! But later when the same person speaks gibberish in a church, they expect that to be interpreted by another person; otherwise, he should keep his mouth shut! They say Jesus is God the Father. They also believe that the Holy Spirit is the Father of Jesus! Therefore, one can say a strong delusion began in the US when this movement sarted. It led to Dispensational theology which is nothing but a delusion, so also Oneness doctrine! I had close discussion for years with a staunch Pentecostal lady believing in this cultish denomination. She is used to behave like the one possessed!

These people have the use of two tongues, one known and another unknown—a kind of split tongue found in serpents! It represents Satan who appeared to Eve as a serpent! It is plain double speaking! Their behaviour also appears to be in tune with that—in and outside church differently!

Million of Pentecostals and Charismatics (not to mention other Protestant and Catholic tongue speakers) claim to possess a gift from God which enables them to "speak in unknown tongues." What is the Scriptural truth regarding this popular Christian doctrine which is claimed to be a primary proof that one either does or does not possess God's Holy Spirit?

At the Pentecost, the Holy Spirit motivated people to speak a known foreign language unknown to them. But the unknown tongue is that of the person speaking and it is nothing to do with the Holy Spirit. None other than Paul said so: "For if I pray in an unknown tongue, my spirit prayeth, but my understanding is unfruitful" (1 Corinthians 14:14). But, unfortunately, deluded people are unable to understand that; as images of God, we too have three aspects, namely, body, spirit and soul! Paul also pointed out that when praying with unknown tongue (gibberish) our mind would be unfruitful. That means, it is coming in the way of bearing the fruit of the Spirit which is a must for our salvation! One may not utilize the gift, but bearing fruit is his responsibility as one abides with Christ.

1 John 4:1 tells us: "Beloved, believe not every spirit, but try the spirits whether they are of God: because many false prophets are gone out into the world."

It has been observed in Pentecostal churches, after one spoke an unknown tongue, one may interpret, but if another interpreter is allowed he would be giving a different version altogether! So one can see that the gibberish speaking is a faking 'spirit-filled' status while the other is interpreting fraudulently—both delusions!

In their argument, perhaps, they deliberately mix up person's spirit with that of the Holy Spirit by using 'S' instead of 's'! I have seen them play this mischief by using upper case letters whenever the word 'spirit' is mentioned, like, writing 'SPIRIT' as if to highlight their arguments! Actually we know the difference between 'spirit' and 'Spirit'. This they want to hide surreptitiously!

Of the 20 times "tongues" is used with reference to a gift from God in the NT, there are only three examples of anyone actually speaking in another language: one in Acts 2:7 to 11; two in Acts 10:46 and three in Acts 19:6. In all these cases they spoke of 'wonderful works of God in the first instance, and they heard 'God magnified' in the second instance followed by 'prophesied' in the third instance, nothing like gibberish (unknown tongue) talk that needed translation or interpretation.

There are no other examples of anyone supernaturally speaking in a language, in all Scripture. If that happens again, then it is an example of the Holy Spirit speaking through them. Otherwise, it is plain rubbish!

The King James term "*unknown* tongue» with addition of the word 'unknown' stands for any utterance that needs an interpreter to understand it. Actually the word 'unknown' is not found in the Greek manuscript but added for clarification.

So clearly the disciples spoke in languages on Pentecost, and thereafter we have two examples of Gentiles speaking in languages. All remaining references to languages (as a gift from God) are discussed by Paul in I Cor. 12, 13, and 14, and nowhere else.

The statement in Mark 16:17, which states in part: "… they shall speak with new tongues" is part of what is called, "The Longer Ending of Mark," and is not found among the oldest Greek Manuscripts. Others contain it, but make notation that it is "questionable." Even if that were to be considered, it indicates speaking of new foreign languages unknown to them but understood by some people present! It is not unknown (gibberish) tongue anyway! That is like a fellow who had no knowledge of English going to USA and speaking English (new tongue for him) that is understandable by the people there!

Paul said, "If any men speak in an *unknown* tongue, *let it be* by two, or at the most *by* three, and *that* by course; and let one interpret. But if there be no interpreter, let him keep silence in the church; and let him speak to himself, and to God" (I Cor. 14:27-28).

This is Paul's tall order! If we assumed that people speak an unknown tongue are prompted by the Holy Spirit, how can any person have the right to suggest him to keep silent? God will not waste His word go unnoticed nor return to Him doing nothing! This proves that the unknown tongue is an utterance of an emotional person!

"But the manifestation of the Spirit is given to every man to profit withal" (1 Corinthians 12: 7).

There must be a "profit" or "contribution to all", from these gifts. Therefore, speaking in an unknown language is never ever to be a physical spectacle for self-aggrandizement of the flesh. Nowhere else in the Bible have we found a case of the Holy Spirit seeking a third party to interpret for Him!

Paul lists spiritual gifts at three different places, namely, in 1 Corinthians, Romans and Ephesians. Only in 1 Corinthians 12:10 he spoke of tongues that needed interpreter something that is not found in Romans and Ephesians. Here are the verses that do not indicate of 'tongue speaking' mentioned by Paul:

"Having then gifts differing according to the grace that is given to us, whether prophecy, *let us prophesy* according to the proportion of faith; Or ministry, *let us wait* on *our* ministering: or he that teacheth, on teaching; Or he that exhorteth, on exhortation: he that giveth, *let him do it* with simplicity; he that ruleth, with diligence; he that sheweth mercy, with cheerfulness" (Romans 12:6); and "Wherefore he saith, When he ascended up on high, he led captivity captive, and gave gifts unto men······And he gave some, apostles; and some, prophets; and some, evangelists; and some, pastors and teachers" (Ephesians 4:8 & 11).

These two letters were written after 1 Corinthians. Do these indicate that Paul was spiritually growing, and he did not want to identify speaking in unknown tongue with interpretation as some kind of spiritual gift subsequently?

Therefore, it is amply clear that strange tongue speaking was limited to the infamous Corinthian church for which he came up with a temporary solution recommending desiring greater gifts with a hope that they would heed his advice and grow spiritually to get over that emotional exhibitionism! Fortunately, it did disappear in the course of time. Basically, Paul again used his craftiness with a 'white lie' to solve this ungainly behaviour! That is, speaking gibberish and interpretation are not part of spiritual gifts. They were included solely to take care of the local problem at Corinth using pragmatism by Paul. However, Satan is still ruling this evil world, and raised his ugly head at an opportune time again!

In I Cor. 12:29-30, we are told something amazing—something that totally contradicts the tongues-speakers' claim that the gift of speaking in languages is absolutely necessary as a proof that one actually has God's Holy Spirit:

"Are all apostles? Are all prophets? Are all teachers? Are all workers of miracles? Have all the gifts of healing? Do all speak with languages? Do all interpret?" (Verse 29-30.)

Many deluded Pentecostal Christians think that Paul was speaking in angelic tongues! Paul simply said what if he did speak angelic voice, not that he spoke as can be made out from this verse:

"Though I speak with the tongues of men and of angels, and have not charity, I am become *as* sounding brass, or a tinkling cymbal" (1 Corinthians 13:1). The key word to understand this verse is 'Though'. Man can never speak like angels! We are more than angels after we enter heaven and be there!

Paul never spoke in unknown tongue in a church. We are not bothered about what one speaks inside the four walls of one's room! He asked Corinthians to desire better gifts than speaking in unknown tongue. One can easily deduce that, with the attitude of Paul trying to give a long rope before asking for a change, Paul played his tricks of being with them with a hope of bringing in a change. There is nothing like an unknown tongue for the Holy Spirit! Only immature people will indulge in emotional cards as Paul hinted at them:

"And I, brethren, could not speak unto you as unto spiritual, but as unto carnal, *even* as unto babes in Christ. I have fed you with milk, and not with meat: for hitherto ye were not able *to bear it,* neither yet now are ye able. For ye are yet carnal: for whereas *there is* among you envying, and strife, and divisions, are ye not carnal, and walk as men?" (1Corinthians 3:1 to 3).

Here is a testimony of a truth seeker when he attended a Pentecostal church:

"Twenty years ago I attended several weekly Sunday services in a very large Atlanta Pentecostal Church, which was replete with a full philharmonic orchestra. It was a beautiful church. And each week at least one person would burst out in an "unknown" tongue. I say, "Unknown," for truly this was not the language of any people on this earth.

In each case, the lead Pastor pretended to interpret what the tongue-speaker had babbled. I acquired a tape of the day's service, and I listened to both the speaker and the interpreter over and over, very carefully. The tongues-speaker started with a long rhythmical phrase which was precisely repeated several times throughout her exhibition. The Pastor then interpreted. He had a very precise interpretation for the first long rhythmical phrase, and although this same phrase repeated itself several more times, the Pastor never gave it the same interpretation as in the opening phrase. Hmmm?"

Jesus should be our perfect Model. He did not speak in an unknown tongue, so also all the chosen apostles. Let me reiterate again that Paul was not a chosen 'apostle' in Jesus' earthly ministry or later!

Now here we have a real spiritual accomplishment: a sinner coming to true repentance and acknowledging the goodness of God. And what has brought about this accomplishment of God's Spirit? Speaking in unknown languages? Certainly not! Prophesying or speaking the inspired word of God with the understanding of the mind, that's what. But today's tongue-talkers don't even speak in *genos (Greek word)* languages. Does anyone really believe that chattering jabbers of gobbledygook, sputtering stammering stutter, or babbling a bunch of burble, will truly convert anyone?

Even though Paul commands that no one should speak in an unknown tongue in the church without an interpreter, it is very common to see speakers and pastors of Pentecostal churches suddenly utter gibberish words frequently and briefly as they proceed to give messages without translating what those words meant! Obviously, they do not know for themselves their meanings! Who do they believe actually? It is free for all circus-shows most of the time!

"And the spirits of the prophets are subject to the prophets. For God is not *the author* of confusion, but of peace, as in all churches of the saints" (1 Corinthians 14:32, 33).

From the above verse one can make out that unknown tongue was spoken by the spirits of the prophets, not the Holy Spirit, who is One! The confusion and noise created in Pentecostal and Charismatic churches prove that God will remain outside of such churches unable to bear their loud clapping and shouts! Or it may mean that people themselves are subject to their spirits that control their shameful exhibitions!

It is common to see people falling backwards in such churches and congregations! Godly people were found to fall on their faces as can be seen in Genesis 17:3 and Jesus in Matthew 26:39.

Who ever heard of "falling over backward" to pay homage to a dignitary? Why, such an abomination is 'not so much as named among the Gentiles,' that one should blaspheme God in paying homage by falling over backward in His presence! Just who is "subject" to whom, in such a disgusting carnival sideshow exhibition of the flesh?

But isn't there a verse that says something about the Spirit helping us praying with "groanings?" Isn't this a form of talking in "*unknown* tongues?» Absolutely not! Let's read the verse:

"Likewise the Spirit also helpeth our infirmities: for we know not what we should pray for as we ought: but the Spirit itself maketh intercession for us with groanings which cannot be uttered" (Romans 8:26).

It is not the Holy Spirit groaning, it is the person praying that is groaning finding no words to express! This can be seen on what Paul said on creatures groaning in the earlier verses:

"For we know that the whole creation groans and suffers the pains of childbirth together until now. And not only this, but also we ourselves, having the first fruits of the Spirit, even we ourselves groan within ourselves, waiting eagerly for *our* adoption as sons, the redemption of our body" (Romans 8:22,23).

And never confuse "spiritual gifts" with "fruit of the Spirit": for the "fruit of the Spirit" is higher than the "spiritual gifts" than the heavens are higher than the earth, for all of the "spiritual gifts" are of the earth, earthy, whereas the "fruit of the Spirit" is truly heavenly. There can be no salvation without the fruit of the Spirit!

One can conclude that speaking in unknown tongue (gibberish) is not a sign of the Holy Spirit, and those who are indulging in that are not glorifying our God! Sign of the indwelling of the Holy Spirit is the fruit (Galatians 5:22, 23). Those who give importance to gifts over the fruit do so at their own peril of losing salvation because God the Father will cut off branches that do not bear fruit though abiding in Jesus (John 15:2). Gifts, if they had not been used for common good, will remain with people worthless from the point of attaining salvation!

Pentecostal and Charismatic groups show all serpentine attributes, such as, double-speaking and split-personality behaviour in and outside the church because they are under delusion by Paul's deviations!

Neither Jesus nor Paul resorted to charismatic techniques to sway the minds of people wrongly with emotional outbursts as can be seen from these verses:

"For they say, 'His letters are weighty and strong, but his personal presence is unimpressive and his speech contemptible'" (2 Corinthians 10:10).

"Who hath believed our report? and to whom is the arm of the LORD revealed? For he shall grow up before him as a tender plant, and as a root out of a dry ground: he hath no form nor comeliness; and when we shall see him, *there is* no beauty that we should desire him. He is despised and rejected of men; a man of sorrows, and acquainted with grief: and we hid as it were *our* faces from him; he was despised, and we esteemed him not" (Isaiah 53:1 to 3).

4

Deviations and Contradictions in Paul's Writings

We have seen that Jesus called Paul to be His 'chosen vessel' to preach the Gospel to all, Jews and others alike. But we also discussed that when it became difficult to preach to the Jews who were well versed in the God's Law, Paul took an easy path of reaching out to Gentiles on his own as can be seen in Acts:13:46 and also in Acts 18:6. After this deviation on his own, Luke records an endorsement for this path only later in Acts 22:21.

In the Great Commission of Jesus (Matthew 28:18-20) disciples were asked to baptize the believers in the name of the Father, the Son and the Holy Spirit. This was specifically commanded to the eleven disciples by the Lord after His resurrection. Of course, Paul was not there. Naturally, he ignores this important directive and stops baptizing the believers assuming he was not called to do that as can be seen from this verse:

"For Christ sent me not to baptize, but to preach the gospel: not with wisdom of words, lest the cross of Christ should be made of none effect" (1 Corinthians 1:17).

It can only be called his presumptions!

We have:

"And call no *man* your father upon the earth: for one is your Father, which is in heaven" (Matthew 23:9).

But Paul assumes that status of father unwittingly in the following verse:

"For though ye have ten thousand instructers in Christ, yet have ye not many fathers: for in Christ Jesus I have begotten you through the gospel" (1 Corinthians 4:15).

You may call this charge as something trivial! How can it be? Can we expect the Paul's writings to supersede the sayings of Jesus? Unfortunately, that is the trend in the Protestant camp in most of the cases!

We find Paul profusely use the word 'saints' in many of his epistles while addressing the congregation of that place. It is not sure whether he was referring to a few members of the church known for their exemplary life of sacrifice and service or to all in the congregation. Catholics give this title to persons when they satisfy certain conditions before and particularly after death. In fact, even Pope is not considered as a saint during his lifetime! Many Protestants come with a liberal belief that all believers are saints. So any Tom, Dick and Harry can pat on his back and claim himself as a saint! We see two extreme positions. The truth ought to lie somewhere in the middle!

In the OT, saints were those who were set apart as the holy ones devoted in the service of God. Therefore, not all Jews were saints that included David, Solomon, et al!

Gospel ought to be preached free, not for a salary. All kinds of evangelists and professional personnel are having a field day in pulling out parts of the verses of Paul to tickle the ears of immature believers to fatten their purses and fill up the coffers of the churches!

We are, without any doubt, sinners. Claiming, ourselves as 'saints' based on Paul epistles, is erroneous. Paul was not an apostle though he claims that way! He was a sinner like all of us, but a saint too for he had given up everything to serve the Lord after his conversion. He was not attempting to raise a family! A saint is both a believer and follower of the Lord taking up the cross daily freed from all encumbrances.

All believers are not saints! There were all kinds of people in the churches founded by Paul. Taking his address as applicable to all believers and all people who were attending the church is self-patting and self-claiming in tune with the claims of Paul!

If sainthood declared by Catholics is based on certain extreme conditions, claim of sainthood by all Protestants is another extreme that is not justified by any means!

Practically—as mentioned before—no one criticizes the Gospel, preaching and practice of Jesus Christ; it is typically on Paul's epistles and on Christendom that is full of nominal Christians who have deviated from the fundamental essence of the Gospel!

Paul speaks of gospel in his epistles, but not a single verse, found in any of the four books of the gospel has been quoted in all of his thirteen epistles! Nevertheless, there are many things that we need to understand for our Christian life in his writings keeping the context in view. He performed his tasks assigned as a 'chosen instrument' to the Gentiles, more or less, effectively using all possible methods! His epistle to Galatians proves that even though it does reflect much of his egoism that remained, perhaps, as a 'thorn in his flesh'. To understand Paul one has to stand on the rock of Peter!

Paul has dominated Protestants! So much so, even the letter to Hebrews is attributed to him. In our church a less learned girl—in terms of the Bible—who was reading the verses assigned to her was referring the second epistle of Peter as 'a letter Paul wrote to second Peter'! My goodness! What an unnecessary monopoly people have allowed Paul to play in their lives ignoring the simple and beautiful messages of the Gospel!

There is another verse in the Bible badly misunderstood and misquoted by the Protestants: "But the righteous man shall live by faith" (Romans 1:17).

They pick out other verses to prove that mere belief in Jesus makes one righteous, and one can live in any manner one likes, indicating that it is just the faith one should have! Nothing is more far off than this from the truth!

"Even though these three men, Noah, Daniel and Job were in its midst, by their own righteousness they could only deliver themselves," declares the Lord GOD" (Ezekiel 14:14). And "even though Noah, Daniel and Job were in its midst, as I live," declares the Lord GOD, "they could not deliver either their son or their daughter; they would deliver only themselves by their righteousness" (v.20).

The above mentioned three persons were declared righteous by God by their faith and attitude (God knew their hearts) even before they proved that by deeds. They did prove by holding on to the faith in all faithfulness despite facing worst conditions.

Therefore, the verse Romans 1:17 indicates that only the 'righteous'—by the standards approved by God—continue to live with full faith no matter what happens or what is happening all around them! Obviously, righteousness does not come from mere belief! The characteristic of righteous people will be like that of Noah who built a ship on a dry land, far away from any river and sea and who did not identify himself with wicked people of his time; it will be that of Job who never cursed God for his predicament; like that of Daniel who refused to accept paganism's favours and instructions! An unrighteous man will give up his faith the moment he faces disasters or undesirable conditions! It is not the case with a righteous person. He continues to trust God and lives by it irrespective of the circumstances and conditions he is living with, trusting fully that he would be blessed eventually!

The best example to understand this verse is by observing the witnessing done by righteous Shadrach, Meshach and Abednego (Daniel 3:17-18). What a great declaration by the faithful servants of God! I love to quote these verses which give courage to the faithful believers in the Almighty God: "If it be *so,* our God whom we serve is able to deliver us from the furnace of blazing fire; and He will deliver us out of your hand, O king. But *even* if *He does* not, let it be known to you, O king, that we are not going to serve your gods or worship the golden image that you have set up."

The Brethren Assembly people love to quote again and again Isaiah 53:5: "But He was pierced through for our transgressions, He was crushed for our iniquities; the chastening for our well-being fell upon Him, and by His scourging we are healed."

They somehow seem to appreciate that with a sense of sadistic satisfaction! It was reported that one little girl asked her dad why this verse is frequently quoted in the services as if to indicate that it is the only important verse available in the entire Bible!

Another favourite verse that is commonly quoted is Romans 8:1: "Therefore there is now no condemnation for those who are in Christ Jesus." They conveniently forget the following (v.4): "so that the requirement of the Law might be fulfilled in us, who do not walk according to the flesh but according to the Spirit," implying that it is important to walk according to the Spirit to avoid condemnation!

Therefore, it may be correct to assume that Paul was referring to a few in the congregation as saints. Saints of Catholics with their selfless and humble life and deeds put self-proclaimed saints of Protestantism to shame in many cases!

It follows, the title of saint cannot be casually applied to all and the sundry! Only Paul has used this title or status for calling others. It could also mean that he was calling the entire congregation to become saints in the way of life and faith, not that they had already become saints with their beliefs. Certain amount of growth in holiness is imperative for the recognition of saintliness. Paul used the word 'saints' when he wrote to Philippines. But in the same congregation he wrote that some are heading towards destruction as can be seen by this verse: "and not in any way terrified by your adversaries, which is to them a proof of perdition, but to you of salvation, and that from God" (Philippians 1:28). No way can these adversaries be termed saints!

Let us see what Jesus called His faithful believers:

"But be not ye called Rabbi: for one is your Master, *even* Christ; and all ye are brethren" and "Neither be ye called masters: for one is your Master, *even* Christ" (Matthew 23:8, 10).

"And I say unto you my friends, Be not afraid of them that kill the body, and after that have no more that they can do" (Luke 12:4).

He called them brothers and friends. Apart from this, no one has called believers 'saints' excepting Paul. What does it indicate? Was Paul trying cleverly to please people with high sounding titles in return for recognizing him as an apostle? Both are superficial if you believed in Paul, not spiritual in any way!

Therefore, it is all the more important to understand Paul and his background before interpreting his epistles that were written from faraway places on many occasions, with problems of that period. No matter what, Paul's writings are not meant to imitate him, but to imitate Jesus Christ! Gospel is the final authority in all matters! Paul made many self-claims that were not accepted!

Every Pauline letter was written to a specific church or place. But not so in case of James, Peter, John, excepting a couple of short letters of John!

Paul in his over enthusiasm to take the Gospel to the Gentiles went to the extent of degrading the Law that was given to Moses by God! To cite an example, let us consider Romans 7:7: "… I would not have come to know sin except through the Law; for I would not have known about coveting if the Law had not said, "*You shall not covet*"."

Unfortunately, man is born sinful and wicked in his heart, and, therefore, it is difficult to agree with Paul on this! With or without law sin has prevailed and motivated people right from Cain's time! It was there in the Garden of Eden too in the form of a serpent! Lust is a powerful urge within every living thing to procreate and sustain. God's law was meant to control it for healthy societal norms to avoid clashes which are common in animal kingdom.

"But sin, taking opportunity through the commandment, produced in me coveting of every kind; for apart from the Law sin is dead" (v.8).

Not again! All men including beasts are having built-in carnality as a result of the fall of Adam. Agape love can only be brought about by the strength supplied by the Saviour! Sin has prevailed after the fall with or without the law! If it had been dead, there was no need for God to give the law to warn the people the consequences of sin!

"I was once alive, apart from the Law; but when the commandment came, sin became alive and I died" (v.9).

Sin was there before, and it continued with new tricks of operation after the Commandments! Commandment did not revive sin as indicated by Paul!

"For sin, taking an opportunity through the commandment, deceived me and through it killed me" (v.11)

The wages of sin is death, but commandment promised avoidance of punishment, if kept. What sin does is nothing to do with the commandment. As a matter fact it opposes the commandment!

Any important doctrine that is developed cannot be based on one single verse or book or author! It should be verified from all angles, particularly with the books of the Gospel, to claim any validity in the light of final revelation through the Son and His chosen apostles who continued with His ministry on earth after His resurrection.

The worst distortion of truth comes from Romans 5:20: "The Law came in so that the transgression would increase; but where sin increased, grace abounded all the more."

Either Paul was wrong or the verse has been mistranslated! As it is, it is mocking at the Law given by none other than God Himself through Moses! Law was given to prevent transgression with an indication of punishment that would follow when broken. Many Christians interpret this conveniently! They think more they sin more will be the grace of God for them! So why not 'sin more to attract more grace' seems to be the shameful driving force and lifestyle for them!

This is exactly what evil monk, Rasputin, of Russia did! He indulged in fornication without any bounds declaring that he would be bestowed with great amount of grace! Of course Paul himself clarifies on this perversion: "And why not say (as we are slanderously reported and as some claim that we say), "Let us do evil that good may come"? Their condemnation is just" (Romans 3:8).

In stark contrast, we have an incident recorded in Buddhist literature. A young and beautiful prostitute wanted to seduce a young handsome Buddhist monk. It was spurned firmly by the monk. However, after several years when the prostitute became old and sick, the same monk attends to her—without being asked—to help her recover from sickness and agony, naturally, without any carnal desire for her!

Peter clearly noticed how Paul's writings were conveniently interpreted to distort the truth of the message of the Gospel. He wrote, "As also in all *his* letters, speaking in them of these things, in which are some things hard to understand, which the untaught and unstable distort, as *they do* also the rest of the Scriptures, to their own destruction" (II Peter 3: 16).

Concepts and theories, such as, once-saved-is-always-saved (OSAS), imputed righteousness, and deductions based on verses related to foreknowledge, predestination, etc. are something that Jesus did not elaborate on, nor bother about! I think, such theories are required basically for people who want to be continuously reassured over and over again that whatever they do, they should have the guarantee of salvation!

Final judgment will not be like a court wherein one puts forth his arguments to defend his deeds! Such complex theories are the indulgences of people who have their bellies full, and who want to exercise their limited intellect on spiritual matters to their satisfaction!

We need to approach the judgment seat with innocence like a child, and not claiming an intellectual understanding as that of a scholar. When a person accepts the life and teaching of Jesus Christ, it gets him a credit of righteousness. It should be followed by a life of obedience and practice. You are a friend to Him if you obeyed!

Between two people, one who says that he does not have to do good works because he has been saved, and the other who says that he does good works because he has been saved; it is easy to see who is really acknowledging and enjoying the saving grace, obviously the latter!

"I know your deeds, that you are neither cold nor hot; I wish that you were cold or hot. So because you are lukewarm, and neither hot nor cold, I will spit you out of My mouth" (Revelation 3:15-16).

Neither had I to worry about how much money I have in my pocket nor my physical strength to make an arduous pilgrimage to get His blessings and answer to my prayers! He will not forsake us as long as we remain humble and trying to move in the direction that is towards perfection and holiness. Not by statements and declarations but by practice! A symbolic singing of the hymn 'I surrender all' keeping our pockets full with money and holding on to our possessions is pure hypocrisy! Such a realization of a lacunae itself is a righteous thought! That means that we are not demanding salvation on our terms and conditions!

We should be after salvation, not after goodies, possessions, or comforts that are temporal in the world!

Miracles, curing from sickness, etc. are not stepping stones to salvation! Such phenomena are observed and experienced in other religions too! Lazarus who was raised from death by Jesus died subsequently later! If he had not kept the faith in Jesus with fruit of the Spirit, he would not have been saved too later! All these signs are for unbelieving people to get an opportunity to lead a righteous life believing in a true, impartial and faithful God who will offer eternal life subsequently.

5

Distorted Interpretations

Much water has flown under the bridge with the verse of Paul in Romans that indicated, “The just shall live by faith.” (For therein is the righteousness of God revealed from faith to faith: as it is written, the just shall live by faith-- Romans 1:17) This became the banner of understanding for Martin Luther to pursue his life severed from Catholicism. Paul’s letter to Roman was written much later after James wrote his with the words, “Faith without works is dead!” This is in direct opposition to that of Paul in the way people understand it. Opposing tendency and creating division by Paul appear to have continued for a long time. Let us see what can be made out of Paul’s thinking on this since ‘ear tickling’ theories have been made out of this.

Paul quoted this statement from Habakkuk (“Behold, his soul which is lifted up is not upright in him: but the just shall live by his faith” Habakkuk 2:4). The context here was that even when the wicked thrive, it would not perturb a just (righteous) man, and he will continue to live keeping his faith intact with God no matter how miserable his conditions are going to be! It is better translated as ‘the just shall live by his faithfulness’! It is similar to what Job expressed, “Though he slay me, yet will I trust in him: but I will maintain mine own ways before him” (Job 13:15).

Unfortunately, a convenient concept has been built on this with a saying that mere faith is all that is required! To claim further advantage, complacent people have come up with a theology that belief in Jesus will impute justness in them! The concept of imputed righteousness has been built using the verses of Paul to make things easy for nominal Christians.

Imputed righteousness has no value if it is not followed by work of obedience. One may be recognized as a soldier, but that is not of any value if he refuses to fight against the enemy!

This has been clearly clarified by James. Since Martin Luther was for a nominal type of righteousness (a kind of virtual reality), he wanted the letter of James to be excluded from canon of the Bible! He also wanted to remove book of Hebrews because another convenient concept of 'Once saved is always saved' will not find support in that!

The concept 'once saved is always saved' (In short form, OSAS) is very much against the preaching of Jesus. The Lord has clearly said that suffering is part of the faith and one has to endure till the end in order to be saved. These verses make that amply clear:

"And have no root in themselves, and so endure but for a time: afterward, when affliction or persecution ariseth for the word's sake, immediately they are offended" (Mark 4:17), and

"and ye shall be hated of all men for my name's sake: but he that shall endure unto the end, the same shall be saved" (Mark 13:13).

Again unfortunately, people want easy religion with its dogmas and doctrines, and for that Paul's epistles come in handy! Martin Luther also wanted the book of Revelation not be a part of the canon probably because it clarifies that those who claim apostleship on their own are liars, and we know for sure who did that glaringly for all to see!

The claim of imputed righteousness may as well be considered parallel to 'wolf in sheep's skin' analogy!

The great apostle, Peter, had this approach and admiration for the Lord:

"When Simon Peter saw it, he fell down at Jesus' knees, saying, Depart from me; for I am a sinful man, O Lord" (Luke 5:8).

He was the only one who had the courage to walk on water before he started sinking only to be pulled up by the Saviour.

He was the one who did not want Christ to suffer and die only to be rebuked by Jesus.

He was the only one who refused to have his feet washed by Jesus because of his reverence for the Lord till the act was clarified.

He was the only one who followed Jesus later as he had promised when the Lord was taken captive.

He was the only one to have asked for crucifixion upside down since he did not want to equate that to that of the Lord.

I don't see anywhere with a self-claim of imputed righteousness by him!

Do hypocrites want salvation packages, only when it comes with human warranty for a life time?

Defenders of 'imputed righteousness' concept quote these of Paul:

"Even as David also describeth the blessedness of the man, unto whom God imputeth righteousness without works, saying,

blessed are they whose iniquities are forgiven, and whose sins are covered" (Romans 4:6,7); and "Now it was not written for his sake alone, that it was imputed to him; but for us also, to whom it shall be imputed, if we believe on him that raised up Jesus our Lord from the dead" (*Romans 4:23,24).*

But we see here that imputing is not done no matter what, it is done only to those who believe in God which in itself classify one as righteous. But it does not end there. They should prove their faith in God in obeying His directive. This can be seen in this verse also:

"And the scripture was fulfilled which saith, Abraham believed God, and it was imputed unto him for righteousness: and he was called the Friend of God" (James 2:23).

Yes, only God can save. But hypocrites believe that they have been saved already with no signs of the fruit of the Spirit and transformation in their lives! Did not Abraham prove his faith by his obedience?

Protestant Christians have the tendency to claim that they are saved and will never lose that! That is self-proclamation! It is like saying that I know that I love that princess, and I will never lose that feeling! Only thing is that she should agree to marry me! That is 50% percent surety of marriage!

Every verse ought to be understood with proper context and people. That was why Jesus did not stipulate certain books and writings to guide us to truth. It is the Holy Spirit that guides us, not the letters that can be manipulated and interpreted! Convenient concepts start flooding the gates of religions when the founder goes away! Something that holds good for all religions!

One or couple of words used by a person cannot form a core belief leading to a theological concept!

People say that they are saved by faith, and not by their own merit or works and quote Isaiah out of context:

"But we are all as an unclean thing, and all our righteousnesses are as filthy rags; and we all do fade as a leaf; and our iniquities, like the wind, have taken us away" (Isaiah 64:6).

Unfortunately, they forget their responsibilities as believers. Let me remind them the verse of Paul who they consider equal to Jesus to convince them:

"Bear one another's burdens, and thereby fulfill the law of Christ" (Galatians 6:2).

Nominal Christians may think that what 'Good Samaritan' did was improper and a filthy work and what a Levite and priest did was a righteous deed that was commendable! God forbid such a thought! What they fail to realize is that Abraham's faith in God was not imputed to him! He chose to believe. Being a man of free-will, he could have walked out the other way in disobedience!

I am trying to know more about the truth, but understand my depravity, and fear God hoping for salvation with humility! I don't get a free pass over here to enter heaven by meeting the human obligations and expectations!

Jesus did not come to call the righteous! He could have come and walked to the cross for our salvation as many seem to imply. He was here for about three and a half years of preaching the way, life and the truth. That cannot be condensed to a simple easy formula based on a verse of Paul!

I have no hesitation to quote Paul if it fits as truth. How dare one accept a 'chosen vessel' as an apostle? Who gives us salvation? Have we kept Jesus' words and given credence to His preaching?

God wrote only once, that is Ten Commandments! The rest is men's. Jesus said that Moses wrote divorce laws due to the hardness on the part of men! Many seem to cling to false doctrines and creeds with opinions mostly based on them!

God did not tell Paul to write letters! Men with vested interests and power decided on the books as can be seen if one looked at the history of canon. That gives a true perspective of its bad background with Marcion doing the elimination and alteration to suit his whims and fancies in the beginning of the formation of canon! A bad seed cannot sprout a good plant!

Many Christians are just simpletons when it comes to the Gospel! They prefer speculative theology of Paul. In fact it fetches them degrees of various shades and colour in 'knowledge factories' for their micro study of Hebrew/Greek letters!

Paul's conversion was based on his own declaration of Jesus pleading with him. What an audacity! Risen Christ is no longer a suffering servant! Stephan came up with a glorified vision of the risen Christ.

Outpouring of grace of God is like rain. You need to harvest it! One cannot be a lazy bum and let go the water down the streets!

One can quote anybody and anything, but the question is can we believe on what they say? Anyone who writes or makes a statement opposing the preaching of Jesus needs to be ignored for the sake of our salvation.

There is only one God. Why different versions then? Which version is true? The Holy Spirit is the One that should teach us from the writings. God is unbiased. Why biased translations? God is one hundred percent perfect. Not so the versions and manuscripts!

Paul has come between Jesus and us by these verses of his:

"Be ye followers of me, even as I also am of Christ" (1 Corinthians 11:1).

"Wherefore I beseech you, be ye followers of me" (1 Corinthians 4:16).

"Brethren, be followers together of me, and mark them which walk so as ye have us for an ensample" (Philippians 3:17).

"Not because we have not power, but to make ourselves an ensample unto you to follow us (2 Thessalonians 3:9).

There is only one Mediator in Jesus between God and us. No one should come in the way and cause loss of focus on Jesus!

Paul was usurping authority tending to glorify himself! That was egoism tormenting him through the messenger of Satan!

"And lest I should be exalted above measure through the abundance of the revelations, there was given to me a thorn in the flesh, the messenger of Satan to buffet me, lest I should be exalted above measure" (2 Corinthians 12:7).

Paul as a babe among apostles and disciples started the first division in the Church. The curse of God has followed since then with no end to divisions and denominations amongst Pauline Christians! Division is Satanic, unity is Christ like!

Typical thinking of Pauline Christians, who imitate him with self-claims, about people who point out Paul's errors is that they assume all the selected books of the Bible are breathed by the Holy Spirit. Obviously, in that case all the biased translations, manipulated and added-and-deleted words can be categorized as breathed by the Spirit!

Paul may not be a bad guy, but his doctrine was against the preaching of Jesus in many cases since he did not know much about the Lord's ministry. As a Christian he should have talked to Peter separately instead of condemning face to face as indicated below:

"But when Peter was come to Antioch, I withstood him to the face, because he was to be blamed" (Galatians 2:11).

He should have talked to him privately and taken steps as advised by Jesus:

"Moreover if thy brother shall trespass against thee, go and tell him his fault between thee and him alone: if he shall hear thee, thou hast gained thy brother. But if he will not hear *thee, then* take with thee one or two more, that in the mouth of two or three witnesses every word may be established. And if he shall neglect to hear them, tell *it* unto the church: but if he neglect to hear the church, let him be unto thee as an heathen man and a publican. (Matthew 18:15 to 17)

Paul never knew the profound path of reconciliation preached by Jesus!

Peter called him a beloved brother, not an apostle. Pauline group is prepared to somersault to grant status of apostle to Paul at any cost!

There is nothing like availability of pure and inspired word of God because all the original manuscripts of both the OT and NT have disappeared along with the earlier Ark of the Covenant!

Many religious Jews sure kept the Law. They might not have committed adultery, but may have harboured a desire for that with neighbour's pretty wife (David did that)! Jesus went further and said one has to keep the Law spiritually which takes care of both the letter and the spirit behind such a Law. Jesus clarified that the very desire for covetousness is sinful! So when you keep the Law spiritually, you will keep the Law by letter also. Such is the spirituality required to enter the kingdom of heaven. Therefore, the letter of the Law is insufficient for pleasing the God through Jesus Christ with His supreme sacrifice.

We need to be righteous by struggling and striving. Of course, through Jesus Christ, it is possible to conquer the temptations and sinful deeds and thought. On our own, it may not be possible. Jesus clearly said that if your eye sins, gouge it out! One cannot become complacent and continue to enjoy the sins of the world hoping that Jesus will blindfold us before we are tempted!

There is none righteous, no not one! That is what people say quoting these verses:

"As it is written, there is none righteous, no, not one" (Romans 3:10); and "The heart *is* deceitful above all *things*, and desperately wicked: who can know it?" (Jeremiah 17:9).

Therefore, camouflaging with human interpretation of imputed privileges is wrong through and through! There are some basic standards that God will accept as righteousness. Hence Abraham, Noah, Job, Lot were found righteous. When Jesus said He came to call not the righteous, it would mean there were righteous people at that time. That was not sufficient though it was alright in the OT times because full revelation had not been given during that period.

Our righteousness will be decided by God, it is not based on a presumption banking on one or two verses!

Now is the question of bearing the fruit of the Spirit, not just external doings, but by inner attitudes.

God's is perfect and holy, and His righteousness cannot be imparted or imputed to imperfect men!

It is no longer the righteousness through the letter of the Law, rather it is spiritual righteousness one obtains with the help of the Saviour through His help by abiding with Him and producing fruit thereof.

"Therefore we ought to give the more earnest heed to the things which we have heard, lest at any time we should let them slip. For if the word spoken by angels was stedfast, and every transgression and disobedience received a just recompence of reward; how shall we escape, if we neglect so great salvation; which at the first began to be spoken by the Lord, and was confirmed unto us by them that heard him" (Hebrews 2: 1 to 3).

Nobody can think like God!

"For My thoughts are not your thoughts, Nor are your ways My ways," declares the LORD" (Isaiah 55:8).

Nobody can escape the curse of the Law if it was transgressed. The OT speaks of rules for relief. The NT stipulates on repentance and faith in Jesus and willing to avoid sinful life. Otherwise, there will be dire consequence with Lord rejecting us: "And then will I profess unto them, I never knew you: depart from me, ye that work iniquity" (Matthew 7: 23).

Salvation is offered for the obedient that are faithful and continue to adhere to the commandments of God!

Those, who do not strive to work out their salvation with fear and trembling and endure to the end, will have no place in the kingdom. (Philippians 2:12)

Job had the right attitude for chastisement:

"Surely it is meet to be said unto God, I have borne chastisement, I will not offend any more" (Job 34:31).

It is God's prerogative to save His chosen people! Many are called but a few will be chosen! Even the chosen may walk away like Judas Iscariot! We have the warning in Hebrews:

"Of how much sorer punishment, suppose ye, shall he be thought worthy, who hath trodden underfoot the Son of God, and hath counted the blood of the covenant, wherewith he was sanctified, an unholy thing, and hath done despite unto the Spirit of grace?" (Hebrews 10:29).

If one considered good works are filthy rags, what about the wicked doings? I leave that to one's imagination!

"Jesus saith unto him, I am the way, the truth, and the life: no man cometh unto the Father, but by me" (John 14:6).

Many nominal Christians may stop at Jesus and may not stand before God!

Jesus was a supreme sacrifice that was total. Does it mean God saves all those who hear this statement?

The fruit of the Spirit is the proof of His dwelling.

"Having your conversation honest among the Gentiles: that, whereas they speak against you as evildoers, they may by your good works, which they shall behold, glorify God in the day of visitation" (1 Peter 2:12).

Spiritual gifts are available to those who will remain obedient and faithful for doing common good. For this

Jesus will baptize with the Holy Spirit. Only He can do it. Baptism of men followed by speaking gibberish is not a proof of baptism by the Holy Spirit. It is a fraudulent claim of deranged people!

Let us not reduce so great a salvation by a single dimensional thinking. It is multifaceted! Please remember it is the way, life and truth that take you to God the Father! Mere faith is dead!

I accept all writings if they compliment the Gospel and preaching of Jesus. Self-claims unsupported by the essence of the preaching of Christ and His apostles ought to be rejected. A single source, verse, author and book cannot form a basis for theological concept. One has to see other sources also. That is the reason why Christendom will not and cannot offer salvation!

Paul is referring 'the deeds of the law' to basically the rituals that became the part of temple worship, and redemption with animal sacrifices. They became no longer sufficient for justification after the supreme sacrifice of Jesus. Law also helps in knowing the sins.

"Wherefore, my brethren, ye also are become dead to the law by the body of Christ; that ye should be married to another, even to him who is raised from the dead, that we should bring forth fruit unto God" (Romans 7:4)

Paul was wrong in saying that we become dead to the law. Indeed we overcome the law! However, Paul rectified this by saying, "That the righteousness of the law might be fulfilled in us, who walk not after the flesh, but after the Spirit" (Romans 8:4).

Christ did not die to the Law; in fact, He was crucified on terms that were against the Law though He kept the Law perfectly!

One cannot bear fruit with lawlessness and undignified manners. We were especially warned by none other than Jesus Himself: "Not every one that saith unto me, Lord, Lord, shall enter into the kingdom of heaven; but he that doeth the will of my Father which is in heaven. Many will say to me in that day, Lord, Lord, have we not prophesied in thy name? and in thy name have cast out devils? and in thy name done many wonderful works? And then will I profess unto them, I never knew you: depart from me, ye that work iniquity" (Matthew 7:21 to 23).

Paul's interpretation is wrong according to following verse:

"For the law of the Spirit of life in Christ Jesus hath made me free from the law of sin and death" (Romans 8:2).

God has never given a law of sin rather it was law to save us from sin! Law gave the knowledge of sin that existed and a way out for that period. Worldly death would follow everyone till the return of Jesus.

The Law was meant for preparations to receive the Son. It was not complete since the time was not ripe for a total enlightenment of the people who were brought out from the slavery. Law was meant for transgressors.

I am above the Law in the sense that I keep the Law in spirit, no longer satisfied with the letter of it! For example: I follow traffic rules of the land whether watched by police or not!

It is applicable for all. One cannot dishonour parents just because of the faith in Christ with thinking that the Ten Commandments are not applicable to him!

Faith and fruit are two sides of the same coin. Absence of any one makes it counterfeit. Only who endures to the end will be saved. (But he that shall endure unto the end, the same shall be saved-- Matthew 24:13)

It is further endorsed by the following verses:

'Therefore remember from where you have fallen, and repent and do the deeds you did at first; or else I am coming to you and will remove your lampstand out of its place— unless you repent. 'Yet this you do have, that you hate the deeds of the Nicolaitans, which I also hate. 'He who has an ear, let him hear what the Spirit says to the churches. To him who overcomes, I will grant to eat of the tree of life which is in the Paradise of God' (Revelation 2:5 to 7), and "So because you are lukewarm, and neither hot nor cold, I will spit you out of My mouth" (Revelation 3:16)

Can anyone receive God's righteousness? A tall order, no doubt! Anyone can experience anything! But the question is whether it is supported by the preaching of Jesus or other sources?

Even Paul cautioned:

"Wherefore, my beloved, as ye have always obeyed, not as in my presence only, but now much more in my absence, work out your own salvation with fear and trembling" (Philippians 2:12), and "but I keep under my body, and bring it into subjection: lest that by any means, when I have preached to others, I myself should be a castaway" (1 Corinthians 9:27).

One's faith needs to be questioned according to the writings especially that have been compiled into a Bible (Catholic or Protestant). Practically, everyone will have his own faith. The question is what is the truth? Jesus said that

He is the truth. Anything that opposes His teaching ought to be questioned and in many cases rejected.

It is the Holy Spirit who helps in discerning the truth when we refer books that have been modified, altered, changed, biased, etc. Let us not go back to the letter of the books instead of spirit behind them.

We need to go back to the Gospel books to know and understand the way, the life and the truth! Easy concepts are being dished out through Paul since the beginning of his writings. For example we have in *Philippians 2:13 –"For it is God which worketh in you both to will and to do of his good pleasure."*

The above verse is commonly quoted to indicate that God will work out our salvation. That is passing the buck of responsibility to God. He will work on a yielding and humbling spirit. In order for the lightning to strike the ground, both the ground and clouds above should have opposite charges accumulated.

So also in the case of salvation: the charge (grace) from above can discharged only when the ground (person) has sufficient opposite charge accumulated for the strike (salvation)!

Unfortunately, Paul wanted his limited gospel to be accepted over what was experienced and learned by the apostles over a period of three and a half years.

Accepting the Saviour is the first step. You have a race to run. You cannot sleep at the first step. Paul's complex theology will contradict his own statement as follows: "But I fear, lest by any means, as the serpent beguiled Eve through his subtilty, so your minds should be corrupted from the simplicity that is in Christ" (2 Corinthians 11:3).

Paul cannot be attributed to have copious flow of the Spirit at the expense of others; no way!

His limited version of the gospel was pushed through sans important essence of the preaching of the Lord.

Paul made too many self-claims and took easy routes to dominate comparatively the semi-literate apostles.

"But Paul said, I am a man which *am a* Jew of Tarsus, a city in Cilicia, a citizen of no mean city: and, I beseech thee, suffer me to speak unto the people" (Acts 21:39).

The above verse shows that Paul was a great opportunist, and he misled the people by claiming that he is still a Jew even after conversion, thereby, denying the Lord before them!

He quotes the Lord as though He was pleading with him to stop persecution in the vision he saw just before conversion. That is not glorified form after ascension! That was Paul's claim! Yes, it has been recorded by Luke only. Paul doesn't mention that in any of his epistles! After ascension, Jesus was no longer a serving and suffering servant! Stephen's vision is trustworthy:

"But being full of the Holy Spirit, he gazed intently into heaven and saw the glory of God, and Jesus standing at the right hand of God; and he said, "Behold, I see the heavens opened up and the Son of Man standing at the right hand of God" (Acts 7:55, 56).

Stephan had seen the suffering Jesus in His earthly ministry. He saw His glory in heaven. That is what we see when He returns. Paul's testimony doesn't glorify Him! It is a reflection of his egocentric nature—a thorn in his flesh!

Paul used pragmatic wisdom with his craftiness. A scholarly writing does not mean that it would indicate the truth! Jesus then really missed out something on that by not writing anything!

Jesus clearly told that He will send the Holy Spirit to testify about Him and the truth, not through Paul, Luke, et al. You know how ingloriously the canon of the Bible was decided by Marcion.

Why that 2nd Peter took a considerable time to get into the Bible canon compared to 1st Peter? In the entire NT, the word Scripture refers to the OT writings.

No one, including Paul, thought that their writings are going to be considered as Scripture! When they wrote, the word Scripture referred to the OT verses.

Canon was decided by people. I am questioning the application of them when many of them were written for specific problems of that age and people. For example Paul wrote to notorious Corinthian church, and one cannot build a theology by listening to one sided conversation! This is where we really require the Holy Spirit to understand Paul or any another writing.

I go by the understanding that the Word of God is Jesus. We need the Holy Spirit to understand the words of the Bible.

Crucifixion of Jesus was an easy thing to publicize! How much Paul shared about the preaching of Jesus? How much of Jesus' words has Paul quoted from the four books of the Gospel? Jesus clearly instructed, "Teaching them to observe all things whatsoever I have commanded you" (Matthew 28:20). He has not quoted a single verse of the preaching of Jesus in all his thirteen epistles exactly as found in the Gospel!

Why should I divert myself from the preaching of Jesus through convenient formulas and man-made doctrines when the Gospel puts things that are easy to understand but difficult to practice? Therefore, justification by faith alone is not acceptable!

When you say you have faith, you need to show by good works, without expecting anything in return, proving yourself that your claim is not counterfeit!

A misleading, ear tickling and convenient theologies are made out entirely by Paul's epistles. Empty vessels make much noise!

With regard to Peter's mention of Paul's writings along with the word 'Scripture',

I am quoting from "New Bible Commentary" (III Edition) Editors: D. Guthrie, B.D., M.T.H., PhD (formerly Lecturer in New Testament, London Bible College), J.A Motyer, M.A., B.D. (Minister of Christ Church, formerly Principal of Trinity College, Bristol); Inter-Varsity Press, Leicester, England; Reprinted 1989: "The other scriptures can be argued, with equal success, as counting Paul's writings included in, or excluded from, Scripture."

Blindly obedient to Paul does not mean obedient to the Gospel! Paul mania is a kind of idolatry too, like, hero worshiping of the present day! Idols representing gods can be altered or modified to suit the likings of people, so also in the case of the words of the Bible!

The Holy Spirit fills up a man in proportion to what he gives up: encumbrances, such as, family, material and personal possessions etc. Otherwise, it is man-made formulas on piece-wise verses! Good works are pointers to salvation, being done despite salvation!

What was happening before canon was finally decided for hundreds of years?

I think Paul told white lies to push his agenda with Gentiles with whatever limited knowledge he had about the Gospel. We need the help of the Holy Spirit to filter out that to understand what is relevant to us!

Many ignorant people assume that Paul was chosen to bring the gospel of grace to us. They say that it was only given to Paul and not to others, and, therefore, Paul's message was not the same as the rest of the apostles.

But with thirteen letters of his, Paul might have repeatedly elaborated on that, but that doesn't mean concept of grace was only given to him! Here are the others that prove otherwise:

John 1

16 For of His fullness we have all received, and grace upon grace.

17 For the Law was given through Moses; grace and truth were realized through Jesus Christ.

Acts 4

33 And with great power the apostles were giving testimony to the resurrection of the Lord Jesus, and abundant grace was upon them all.

Acts 11

23 Then when he arrived and witnessed the grace of God, he rejoiced and began to encourage them all with resolute heart to remain true to the Lord;

Hebrews 4

16 Let us therefore come boldly unto the throne of grace, that we may obtain mercy, and find grace to help in time of need.

Hebrews 10

29 Of how much sorer punishment, suppose ye, shall he be thought worthy, who hath trodden underfoot the Son of God, and hath counted the blood of the covenant, wherewith he was sanctified, an unholy thing, and hath done despite unto the Spirit of grace?

James 4

6 But he giveth more grace. Wherefore he saith, God resisteth the proud, but giveth grace unto the humble.

1 Peter 1

2 Elect according to the foreknowledge of God the Father, through sanctification of the Spirit, unto obedience and sprinkling of the blood of Jesus Christ: Grace unto you, and peace, be multiplied.

10 Of which salvation the prophets have enquired and searched diligently, who prophesied of the grace that should come unto you:

13 Wherefore gird up the loins of your mind, be sober, and hope to the end for the grace that is to be brought unto you at the revelation of Jesus Christ;

1 Peter 3

7 Likewise, ye husbands, dwell with them according to knowledge, giving honour unto the wife, as unto the weaker vessel, and as being heirs together of the grace of life; that your prayers be not hindered.

1 Peter 4

10 As every man hath received the gift, even so minister the same one to another, as good stewards of the manifold grace of God.

1 Peter 5
5 Likewise, ye younger, submit yourselves unto the elder. Yea, all of you be subject one to another, and be clothed with humility: for God resisteth the proud, and giveth grace to the humble.
10 But the God of all grace, who hath called us unto his eternal glory by Christ Jesus, after that ye have suffered a while, make you perfect, stablish, strengthen, settle you.
12 By Silvanus, a faithful brother unto you, as I suppose, I have written briefly, exhorting, and testifying that this is the true grace of God wherein ye stand.
2 Peter 1
2 Grace and peace be multiplied unto you through the knowledge of God, and of Jesus our Lord,
2 Peter 3
18 But grow in grace, and in the knowledge of our Lord and Saviour Jesus Christ. To him be glory both now and for ever. Amen.
2 John 1
3 Grace be with you, mercy, and peace, from God the Father, and from the Lord Jesus Christ, the Son of the Father, in truth and love.
Jude 1
4 For there are certain men crept in unawares, who were before of old ordained to this condemnation, ungodly men, turning the grace of our God into lasciviousness, and denying the only Lord God, and our Lord Jesus Christ.
Revelation 1
4 John to the seven churches which are in Asia: Grace be unto you, and peace, from him which is, and which was, and which is to come; and from the seven Spirits which are before his throne;

Revelation 22
21 The grace of our Lord Jesus Christ be with you all. Amen.

Protestants imitate Paul as advised by him to understand Jesus and Catholics try to reach Him through Mary. Both are starting deviations from the truth that is Jesus!

Peter was the greatest apostle indeed, and he was authorised to carry on the ministry by Jesus Himself.

But most Protestants want to belittle him for two reasons: firstly, to dispute the succession of Pope in his direct line, and secondly to elevate Paul so that his compromise theology can be conveniently adopted, ignoring the Sermon on the Mount and the teachings of Jesus!

Unfortunately, Catholics are blind with their traditions, and Protestants are biased with their translations (interpretation) consequently, the truth is the victim.

Giving respect and regard to Peter does not imply infallibility of Pope!

As a matter of fact, the word 'nepotism' originated from the biased dealings of a Pope! I do not have to mention the violence perpetuated by the Catholic Church on many occasions unreasonably.

Traditions are meant to bring order in the conduct of the service, and they are in no way related to spiritual matters, like, the rituals of the OT!

6

Views of a Truth Seeker

Here are keen and relevant observations of a truth seeker:

"I entered Southern Seminary thinking that this issue would very soon find a resolution. It did not. It only became more intense and prominent as the seminary years progressed. The hard commandments of the Sermon on the Mount increasingly seemed tailor made to my central interests in the violence of Christendom that was World War II. But to my dismay, the Seminary faculty did nothing to relieve my growing concern. A typical response was to assure me that no one could keep those commandments. "They are only meant to convict us of sin so that we will trust in the blood of Jesus for forgiveness." I could never match those assurances with anything from the utterances of Jesus but found them contradicted on every hand.

Martin Luther, inspired by Paul, concluded that the Epistle of James was "an epistle of straw." I, inspired by Jesus and James, have finally concluded that Paul was an *apostle of straw*. I still acknowledge Paul's great zeal for Christ, but it was zeal for a Christ misunderstood. Paul's suffering for Christ bespeaks his great love for him, but it was love for a Christ misconceived. His preaching of Christ was among the most effective the world has ever seen, but it was of a Christ mis-preached. What follows is an effort to present Paul as I have come to know him, minus his halo but yet clothed with a kind of respect that seems at times contradictory, even to me. Seeing Paul, as he really is – warts and all – does not detract from my admiration of the work he performed.

It is very unlikely that any of the early disciples thought of their own writings as scripture, with the possible exception of Paul [*The author doubts even this*]. I will explain this possible exception below. And would Peter have been one who characterized Paul's letters as scripture? Hardly! (This assumes that Peter authored the Petrine epistles, which many doubt. I have no problem with Peter's authorship, provided we allow for redactions such as this.) Could Paul have seen himself as filling the vacancy? No, for he would surely have made that his claim. The fact is that the remaining eleven were instrumental in the selection of Matthias to fill this vacancy as even Luke informs us in The Acts, and had Paul seen himself as being Judas' replacement, Luke would certainly have seen him as such. I believe, nevertheless, that Paul was Judas's successor – as traitor! Judas betrayed him in his flesh; Paul betrayed him in his spirit.

I see him as one who was, at a certain level, a man of great integrity who could persuade and deceive others only because he had first persuaded himself, which contributed to the effectiveness of his ministry. He preached in all sincerity what he really believed. Furthermore, a portion of his doctrine is wonderfully and gloriously true, which renders it all the more deceptive as even Paul could have understood from the standpoint of one who could accuse other "apostles" of disguising themselves as "servants of righteousness" (II Corinthians 11:15).

Now I, Paul, say to you that if you receive circumcision, Christ will be of no advantage to you. I testify again to every man who receives circumcision that he is bound to keep the whole law. You are severed from Christ, you who would be justified by the law; you have fallen away from grace (Galatians 5:2-4).

This is his unequivocal assertion of one of his most basic convictions. But look at what he did:

And he came to Derbe and to Lystra. A disciple was there, named Timothy, the son of a Jewish woman who was a believer; but his father was a Greek. He was well spoken of by the brethren at Lystra and Iconium. Paul wanted Timothy to accompany him; and he took him and circumcised him because of the Jews that were in those places, for they all knew that his father was a Greek (Acts 16:1-3).

If this isn't inconsistency and compromise, I would not know how to define these things. Of course, one could defend Paul here by saying that the Galatian letter was written long after he had Timothy circumcised, and his views matured during the interval. Let us then say that is the case, and look at the implication: His views changed from one thing to another during the period when he was preaching his gospel throughout the world. The Truth, however, did not change during that period, for that is unchanging. He therefore could not have been preaching the Truth during this period of changing views, yet he claimed to be preaching the same gospel from beginning to end. This leaves us with no basis for believing that he ever preached the True Gospel!

Did he really see a bright light? And did he really hear a voice? I believe he did, although it is questionable that others saw or heard them. The contradictions in the accounts of his revelation are sufficient to cause us to question his objectivity at the moment and his veracity afterwards.

In his defence before the Jerusalem crowd as Luke related in Acts 22:9 he said, "Now those who were with me saw the light but did not hear the voice of the one who was speaking to me."

But then Luke described Paul's experience in Chapter 9 thusly: The men who were traveling with him stood speechless, hearing the voice but seeing no one. (Acts 9:7)

Paul claimed that the gospel which was preached by him is not man's gospel, for he said, "I did not receive it from man nor was I taught it, but it came through a revelation of Jesus Christ."

Are we to believe that Jesus communicated directly to Paul the doctrine of his return to earth in Paul's lifetime? He said above, "... this I declare unto you by the word of the Lord." If so, Jesus was also mistaken. But in this case, Jesus can no more be identified with Truth.

I much prefer some other option, such as that Paul was the one mistaken; that he had visions during which he believed he was communicating with Jesus, when he actually was not. He therefore received his gospel, not from Jesus, but from whatever source it was that communicated with him during his visions. This is not the place to expand on the significance of this. Here it is only necessary to demonstrate that Paul could be in error in a case in which we can be certain he erred, for this alone is sufficient to justify our questioning everything he taught about Jesus Christ.

So, Paul's doctrine of Jesus' soon coming was clearly erroneous, being falsified by two thousand years of history Paul quotes at times without any regard to the context in which the passage is found in the Old Testament.

Justification by Faith

Justification by faith only and apart from works of the law can be said to be a major theme of Paul's gospel. Indeed, I suppose this could be said to be his gospel, his good news, in a nutshell. After stating his case in Romans 3, he goes on in Chapter 4 to call forth the example of Abraham to cement his case. A similar argument is also presented in the Galatian letter. Focusing on the statement in Genesis 15:6, "Abraham believed God and it was reckoned to him as righteousness" (or justification), Paul proceeds to set forth the idea that this justification came to Abraham before he was circumcised, and therefore is independent of circumcision so that the uncircumcised Gentiles are as qualified to receive it as are the Jews. Then, secondly, that it is independent of the law or of works of the law. Abraham believed God and had faith in his promise, even in the knowledge of the barrenness of Sarah's womb and his own advanced age. As Paul explained,

No distrust made him waver concerning the promise of God, but he grew strong in his faith as he gave glory to God, fully convinced that God was able to do what he had promised. That is why his faith was "reckoned to him as righteousness" (Rom. 4:20-22).

So it is on this basis that Paul seeks to establish Abraham as the prime example of justification by faith only, and not by works.

This, however, is not the entire story. If we examine the wider contest of Genesis, we must conclude that Abraham's blessing came through both faith and works of law, and especially through the latter. God spoke to Abraham and said,

I will indeed bless you, and I will multiply your descendants as the stars of heaven and as the sand which is on the seashore.

And your descendants shall possess the gate of their enemies, and by your descendants shall all the nations of the earth bless themselves, *because you have obeyed my voice* (Genesis 22:17, 18).

No mention here of faith, only that Abraham obeyed the voice of the Lord – a work of obedience to law! Then, later, when God extended the same blessing to Isaac, it was because Abraham had . . . obeyed my voice and kept my charge, my commandments, my statutes, and my laws. (Genesis 26:5).

So that when Paul wrote, The promise to Abraham and his descendants, that they should inherit the world, did not come through the law but through the righteousness of faith (Romans 4:13), he chose to ignore the full explanation of the Genesis text. To cap it all off, nowhere in Genesis can I find that God promised Abraham that his descendants would inherit the world! He only promised them the Land of Canaan (Genesis 17:8).

The Epistle of James may have been written for the purpose, in part, of countering this "faith only" doctrine of Paul. James also appeals to Abraham, specifically to the offering of Isaac as sacrifice, and concludes, "Do you want to be shown, you foolish fellow, that faith apart from works is barren? Was not Abraham our father justified by works, when he offered his son Isaac upon the altar? You see that faith was active along with his works, and faith was completed by his works, and the scripture was fulfilled which says, "Abraham believed God, and it was reckoned to him as righteousness;" and he was called the friend of God. You see that a man is justified by works and not by faith alone. (James 2:20-24)

He advances a collection of six quotations from various contexts of the Old Testament to put this point, the universality of human sinfulness and depravity, to rest once for all. Let us list them all for closer examination, after which I will comment on each one briefly:

1. Romans : (3:10-12) None is righteous, no, not one; no one understands, no one seeks for God. All have turned aside, together they have gone wrong; no one does good, not even one (Psalm 14:1-3).
2. (3:13a) Their throat is an open grave, they use their tongues to deceive (Psalm 5:9).
3. (3:13b) The venom of asps is under their lips (Psalm 140:3).
4. (3:14) Their mouth is full of curses and bitterness (Psalm 10:7).
5. (3:15-17) Their feet are swift to shed blood, in their paths are ruin and misery, and the way of peace they do not know (Isaiah 59:7, 8).
6. (3:18) There is no fear of God before their eyes (Psalm 36:1).

Psalm 14:1-3 appears on first reading to say exactly what Paul wishes it to say. But if we read the balance of the psalm, it becomes evident that the psalmist did not intend what Paul asserted, for in v. 4 we have the evildoers set apart from my people with a clear distinction made between them. Then in v. 5, these evildoers will be in great terror, for God will be with the generation of the righteous, who are then identified with the poor, but the Lord is his refuge. The Psalm closes with v. 7:

O, that deliverance for Israel would come out of Zion! When the Lord restores the fortunes of his people, Jacob shall rejoice, Israel shall be glad.

Clearly, the Psalmist allows for two categories of human beings, the evildoers and the generation of the righteous, who are identified with Israel in the last verse. The "no, not one" must then refer only to the evildoers who eat up my people as they eat bread, and do not call upon the Lord, presumably Gentiles in contrast to Jacob and Israel. Paul, who seeks by this to prove his point, that all are under condemnation of sin without exception, has not properly regarded the context and has as a result drawn something out of it contrary to the intent of the Psalmist. He has tampered with God's word.

There is no denying it. Paul has here used the Word deceptively. He has tampered with it to make it appear that his position is supported thereby. Not only is this premise not supported by the passages quoted as its support, but neither is it true to the thought of the Old Testament, as Holmes Rolston would have us believe. The thought of the Old Testament, beginning with Cain and Abel, consistently allows for two categories of human beings, the wicked and the righteous, in the manner I have demonstrated above. If Paul's premise is true, it cannot be established by reference to the Law, the Prophets, or the Psalms. Now we know why his opponents charged him with tampering with the Word of God, and why he was compelled to issue denials in his defense.

It is not surprising to see Paul applying this prophecy to the coming of the Christ (Messiah) in the work of Jesus. This is a common application, but he interprets the word for faithfulness as faith, applying it to the conviction of the truth of the redemptive work of Christ, which is not justified when its context is considered. The Septuagint similarly errs in using the Greek, *pistis*, to translate the Hebrew word, for this does mean faith, as Paul understood it.

Since Paul was using the Septuagint, this may explain how he came to misunderstand the word in its context. And he made it the cornerstone of his gospel so it looks suspiciously like he has again been found tampering with God's Word. This is only one more of the numerous incidents where it can be shown that Paul used the Word deceptively.

The Curse

Another prominent feature of his gospel, related to the above postulate that all men are wicked without exception, is the idea of the curse of the law. Writing to the Galatian churches Paul asserted:

For all who rely on the works of the law are under a curse, for it is written, "Cursed be everyone who does not abide by all things written in the book of the law, and do them" (Deuteronomy 27:26, Galatians 3:10).

Then he goes on to say:

Christ has redeemed us from the curse of the law, having become a curse for us – for it is written, "Cursed be everyone who hangs on a tree" (Deuteronomy 21:23) – that in Christ Jesus the blessing of Abraham might come upon the Gentiles, that we might receive the promise of the Spirit through faith (Galatians 3:13-14).

But when we turn to examine the passage cited from Deuteronomy 27:26, we find a much different thought – indeed, a thought that is the opposite of what Paul is attempting to demonstrate. Rather than being under a curse by relying on the works of the law, Moses is establishing only that the curse comes from not doing the words of the law:

Cursed be he who does not confirm the words of this law by doing them (Deuteronomy 26:27).

In fact, Deuteronomy 28:1 pronounces a blessing on all who are careful to do all the commandments of the law. The emphasis on the blessing is clear, for it is extended to cover everyone in all circumstances:

Blessed shall you be in the city and blessed shall you be in the field. Blessed shall be the fruit of your body and the fruit of your ground and the fruit of your beasts, the increase of your cattle, and the young of your flock. Blessed shall be your basket and your kneading-trough. Blessed shall you be when you come in, and blessed shall you be when you go out.

And on and on goes the text, defining the blessing on those who keep the law, who live by it and do it. It is only those who do not obey the voice of the Lord on whom the curses fall (Deuteronomy. 28:15f). In this text, the law is not a curse within itself, nor are all that rely on the works of the law under a curse. Rather, those who obey it are under a manifold blessing!

Paul tampered with God's word? How can this be, seeing that whatever Paul wrote was and is God's word! Did he not himself make the claim that his words were really God's (or "the Lord's, I Thessalonians 2:13, I Corinthians 14:37)? Regarding those sharing this point of view, I can honestly say that my conscience is free. I have done my best to strip you of the church-applied shackles that bind your heart and soul, but if you persist in keeping your head immersed in the sand of Paul's baseless theological speculations, what more can I do?

I can do a great deal more. For one thing, I can provide additional support by demonstrating that Paul was capable of errors in logic. If his inspiration truly came from the Holy Spirit, if he wrote the Word of God in recording his epistles, he surely would not have written or said anything stupid – would he?

The Cretans

The first is his self referential statement in the letter to Titus. Titus had been left in Crete to attend to missionary tasks, and Paul later wrote to him to more clearly define his duties. Early in this letter, referring to the Cretans, he came forth with this astonishing statement:

One of themselves, a prophet of their own said, "Cretans are always liars, evil beasts, lazy gluttons." This testimony is true (Titus 1:12).

But, if Cretans are *always* liars, this statement by one of them must be false. Paul says it is true. Paul has surely fallen into a trap of his own making. If the illogic is not obvious to you, perhaps it will help if I present it as follows, keeping in mind that the Cretan whom Paul was quoting is Epimenides.

1. Paul writes that Epimenides says that Cretans are always liars.
2. Epimenides was a Cretan (a prophet of their own).
3. Therefore Epimenides always lies.
4. Paul says that what Epimenides said is true.

This is a pure conundrum. It is nonsense. Paul says that Epimenides' testimony is true, the very testimony that says that Epimenides is a liar! Surely this kind of puny logic must have a merely human origin, the mind of Paul.

Call No Man Father

I have pointed above to an incident in which Paul calls God to witness to his truthfulness; he did this not once but repeatedly, all in direct disobedience to the commandment of Jesus: "Swear not at all." Here are more examples of disobedience:

Jesus said, Call no man your father on earth, for you have one Father, who is in heaven (Matthew 23:9).

Paul committed, or taught others to commit, several infractions of this commandment, not only continuing to refer to the Patriarchs as "father", but even establishing himself as the father of his converts. The most specific evidence of this comes from I Corinthians. I should tell you that he does not actually title himself "father" in this verse, but the language makes this the necessary interpretation. He actually says,

"I write not these things to shame you, but as my beloved sons I warn *you*. For though ye have ten thousand instructers in Christ, yet *have ye* not many fathers: for in Christ Jesus I have begotten you through the gospel" (1 Corinthians 4:14, 15).

He is teaching Timothy and all his disciples to call him "Father," contrary to the commandment of the Lord in Matthew 23:9! He would have them disobey the Lord.

Then, in Romans 4:16, he speaks of Abraham as the father of us all. He therefore calls Abraham, who was a man on earth, his father, and encourages all other to do so!

You are not to be Called "Teacher"

Jesus commanded, from the same context as above, "But you are not to be called rabbi (teacher), for you have one teacher (didaskalos), and you are all brethren" (Matthew 23:8).

Ignoring this command completely, Paul wrote to the Corinthians, defining the different offices in the church:"And God has appointed in the church first apostles, second prophets, third teachers (didaskalos)" (I Corinthians 12:28).

Then, in both letters to Timothy, he specified his own appointment as preacher, apostle, and teacher (I Timothy 2:7, II Timothy 1:11). This is actually a very good indicator that Paul authored these two letters, though the scholars do not generally accept this. But is God going to appoint anyone as teacher, when his spokesman, Jesus has expressly forbidden that we should be called such?

Go Into Your Room and Shut Your Door

Jesus commanded, "But when you pray, go into your room and shut the door and pray to your Father who is in secret; and your Father who sees in secret will reward you" (Matthew 6:6).

Paul obviously ignored this command, as revealed in his instruction to the Corinthian church concerning public worship: "What am I to do? I will pray with the spirit and I will pray with the mind also; I will sing with the spirit and I will sing with the mind also. Otherwise, if you bless with the spirit, how can anyone in the position of an outsider say the "Amen" to your thanksgiving when he does not know what you are saying?"

It is clear that Paul's disciples engaged in public prayer in their worship together, even as those whom Jesus called "hypocrites" loved to stand praying in the synagogue. Of course, we know of no church that pays any attention to Jesus in this matter, but that should not surprise us. They haven't given him much attention in anything crucial to their salvation. They are much distracted through listening to Paul!

A Witness Needed!

If it is a lie, and you accuse me of lying, I will be forced to respond with a denial because a lie cannot and will not speak for itself. The things that motivated me to lie will motivate me to deny my lie. Then, feeling the weakness of my position, I look for something more! What more can I do? I must call forth a witness, so that you have not only my testimony, but also that of another. The scripture plainly states that everything is established at the mouth of two or three witnesses. You may have me pegged for a liar, but perhaps you will believe someone else. But on whom can I call on such short notice? To be effective, I must have a witness now! Not only so, but my witness must be a person of undisputed veracity, for it will not do to call on a reputed liar. Whose testimony would you accept immediately without question? Who? Who? Who?

Ah! There is only one person right for my task . . . God in heaven! His veracity is beyond question and He carries the extra advantage of never having been known to testify. He would surely condemn me for a liar if He were to testify but, since he never has, I am safe in calling upon him and the very mention of his name may be persuasive.

The God and Father of the Lord Jesus, he who is blessed forever, knows that I do not lie. At Damascus, the governor under King Aretas guarded the city of Damascus in order to seize me, but I was let down in a basket through a window in the wall, and escaped his hands (II Corinthians. 11:31-33).

[The author would like to add that Paul was mentioning the name of the Father and Jesus to prove that he did not lie!

This is something similar in manner to taking vows or swearing which was forbidden by Jesus in Matthew 5:33-37]

But when he who had set me apart before I was born, and had called me through his grace, was pleased to reveal his Son to me, in order that I might preach him among the Gentiles, I did not confer with flesh and blood, nor did I go up to Jerusalem to those who were apostles before me, but I went away into Arabia; and again I returned to Damascus. Then after three years I went up to Jerusalem to visit Cephas, and remained with him fifteen days. But I saw none of the other apostles except James the Lord's brother. In what I am writing to you, before God, I do not lie! (Galatians 1:15-20)

For this I was appointed a preacher and apostle (I am telling the truth, I am not lying), a teacher of the gentiles in faith and truth (I Timothy 2:7).

I am speaking the truth in Christ; I am not lying; my conscience bears witness in the Holy Spirit that I have great sorrow and unceasing anguish in my heart. For I could wish that I myself were accursed and cut off from Christ for the sake of my brethren, my kinsmen by race (Romans 9:1-3).

I count four times here, in the New Testament epistles, that Paul denied that he was lying: to the Corinthians, the Galatians, Timothy, and the Romans. Once, to the Romans, he called the Holy Spirit to witness for him. Twice, to the Corinthians and to the Galatians, he called God to witness for him. Three times, to the Corinthians, Galatians, and to Timothy, the denials were issued concerning his assertions of his calling and apostleship.

His Most Unfavorable Witness

Paul lied. But now I must tell you that Paul did have a witness as to his integrity, and it was not a favorable witness. This was Paul himself:

For though I am free from all men, I have made myself a slave to all, that I might win the more. To the Jews I became as a Jew, in order to win Jews; to those under the law I became as one under the law – though not being myself under the law – that I might win those under the law. To those outside the law I became as one outside the law – not being without law toward God but under the law of Christ – that I might win those outside the law. To the weak I became weak, that I might win the weak. I have become all things to all men, that I might by all means save some. I do it all for the sake of the gospel, that I may share in its blessings. (I Corinthians. 9:19-25).

What a marvelous expression of total commitment to winning souls! I once found this to be one of the most inspiring and motivating passages in the Bible. It made me just want to go out and win souls – to do anything or be anything to accomplish results.

But look closer – he openly acknowledged a practice that is utterly dishonest. To the Jews, he presented himself as a Jew. But to those outside the law, the Greeks and others, he presented himself as outside the law – as a Greek if we go by his Greek name. He became all things to all men! Whatever the occasion demands, that he is. Its begins more and more to appear as though the Ebionites may have been correct in their statements about Paul – that he was a Greek and never a Pharisee Jew. By his own firm statement, he was a human chameleon!

More Than an Apostle

Paul postured not only as an apostle, the greatest of the apostles, but also as more than an apostle. In this he was not prone to subtle concealment of his posturing, but was most straightforward, apparently not realizing what he was doing, but nevertheless revealing the self aggrandizing person he really was. That he could present himself as being the most lowly of apostles, then assert his superiority, betrays hypocrisy that was usually masterfully concealed. In every letter he was careful to affirm his apostolic calling and its divine origin, once emphatically denying that it came through men, but only through Christ by the will of God (Galatians 1: 11, 12). In all except the Thessalonian letters, the one to Philippi, and the personal letter to Philemon, he included this apostolic affirmation in the first line of the letters as I have stated above in the discussion of his office. I list these first lines here once more because they contribute to the conception of his self aggrandizement. Remember: Paul wrote all these lines; there is no one other than him on record as a witness to his high calling. The fact that now, after two millennia, untold millions around the world honor him as an apostle of the Lord only shows how effective a self promoter he really was!

He engaged in self promotion at the beginning of most of his letters:

Paul, an apostle—not from men nor through man, but through Jesus Christ and God the Father, who raised him from the dead—and all the brethren who are with me, To the churches of Galatia: (Galatians 1:1,2).

Paul, called by the will of God to be an apostle of Christ Jesus, and our brother Sosthenes, To the church of God which is at Corinth . . . (I Corinthians 1:1,2).

Paul, and apostle to Jesus Christ by the will of God, and Timothy our brother, To the church of God which is at Corinth: . . . (II Corinthians 1:1).

Paul, a servant of Jesus Christ, called to be an apostle, set apart for the gospel of God which he promised beforehand through his prophets in the holy scriptures . . . Jesus Christ our Lord, through whom we have received grace and apostleship to bring about the obedience of faith for the sake of his name among all nations . . . To all God's beloved in Rome: . . . (Romans 1:1-6).

We must evaluate the character of Paul free from the shackles that the churchmen have clamped upon us. Then he comes through in his true colors. A truly meek and humble man would never boast of his lowliness as Paul often did; a truly meek and humble man would never boast of his superiority, as Paul sometimes did. What others cannot reveal about him because they were silenced long ago, he in his own words reveals about himself.

Paul's Great Failure

I define now the substance of Paul's great failure to adequately comprehend the Gospel. You note how he started by saying that he had delivered to the Corinthians as of first importance what he also received, that Christ died for our sins according to the scriptures. His gospel therefore began with the death of Jesus, and did not draw substantively on anything prior to that. It did not draw on the life of Jesus, or on the gospel that Jesus preached. It did not openly draw on the utterances of Jesus. It was "in accordance with the scriptures" but it was not in accordance with the words of the Lord. If he were standing before me at this moment, he might quickly direct my attention to his assertion that this gospel, which is of first importance, is what "I also received." But this must be read in the light of his statement in Galatians, . . . "the gospel, which was preached by me, is not man's gospel. For I did not receive it from man nor was I taught it, but it came through a revelation of Jesus Christ" (Galatians 1:11,12).

Therefore it did not come from the man, Jesus, but came only from the visions that appeared to Paul and that he identified with the risen Christ. He therefore saw no need of reliance on the utterances of Jesus of Nazareth, and gave little heed to them. Did the risen Christ then repeat the words of Jesus to Paul in his visions? No, for in that case, Paul's gospel would have conformed in every point to that of Jesus. Would the risen Christ have delivered a different message to Paul than he delivered to the disciples as Jesus of Nazareth? No, for Jesus assured us that, though heaven and earth pass away, his word will not pass away. It is therefore, according to Jesus, the permanent and final word from God to men.

I have been careful to note above, many times, that Paul was familiar with the Jesus Tradition, the early record of Jesus' words and deeds. But he drew specifically on this tradition very few times. Indeed, as near as I can tell, he only once drew on words of the Lord that could be definitive of his gospel, but he utilized it to instruct the church in eating and observing the Lords Supper. Since Paul wrote prior to the writing of the gospels, he must have derived these words from the Jesus Tradition, but he claimed that he received them from the Lord (I Corinthians 11:23). As explained above, he meant to be understood as receiving it from the risen Christ, and so in this case failed to credit Jesus of Nazareth."

Certainly, the truth seeker has nailed the speculative, convenient and 'ear tickling' theories based on Paul's epistles for good! A great learned testimony for the truth and for the glorification of Jesus Christ our Lord and Saviour! Amen!

7
Institution of Religion by Paul

Since Paul was not in the earthly ministry of Jesus, he missed out extremely important, profound and sublime preaching of Jesus. He might have learnt a few things about it when he spent some time with Peter in the beginning of his ministry. As expected, he self-proclaimed that Jesus taught him in his vision, hinting, as though the Lord wasted time of about three and a half years earlier with His chosen apostles! With Pharisaic background that relies on oral traditions also along with rituals, he began to assert himself amongst poor semi-literate fishermen who were chosen as apostles by Jesus. Jesus knew that His apostles with their limited knowledge would not be in a position to add any spectacular speculations on their own to His preaching. Jesus chose Paul to tackle knowledgeable Greeks, philosophers of Pagan world and scholarly Gentiles using his worldly scholarship as a tool to identify with them in order to win them over. Unfortunately, Paul exceeded the limits entrusted to him and started monopolising the authority right from the beginning with his questionable visions!

As mentioned earlier, he started the first division in the Church by refusing to give a second chance to Mark in his second missionary journey. From then onwards, practically, he made it a point to oppose all that was understood by the disciples of Jesus. The epistle of James appears to be the first book of the NT. James wrote that faith without good works is dead. Paul comes with a theory that faith alone is sufficient for salvation in his book of Romans; a disputable theory Martin Luther lavishly elaborated!

He directly accosted Peter as indicated in the epistle of Galatians in a manner unbecoming of a Christian though he may be correct in his stand!

Jesus had this to say for the workers of His ministry: "And he called *unto him* the twelve, and began to send them forth by two and two; and gave them power over unclean spirits; and commanded them that they should take nothing for *their* journey, save a staff only; no scrip, no bread, no money in *their* purse: but *be* shod with sandals; and not put on two coats" (Mark 6:7to 8).

On the other hand Paul started salaried class of people for his new religion by telling them, borrowing from the OT standard, "Who goeth a warfare any time at his own charges? Who planteth a vineyard, and eateth not of the fruit thereof? Or who feedeth a flock, and eateth not of the milk of the flock? Say I these things as a man? Or saith not the law the same also?

For it is written in the law of Moses, thou shalt not muzzle the mouth of the ox that treadeth out the corn. Doth God take care for oxen? Or saith he *it* altogether for our sakes? For our sakes, no doubt, *this* is written: that he that ploweth should plow in hope; and that he that thresheth in hope should be partaker of his hope. If we have sown unto you spiritual things, *is it* a great thing if we shall reap your carnal things? (1 Corinthians 9:9 to 11).

Paul coolly mixed up spiritual things with carnal things without even beating his eyelids! Jesus clearly said,"Heal the sick, cleanse the lepers, raise the dead, cast out devils: freely ye have received, freely give" (Matthew 10:8).

So Christianity, instead of becoming a life for disciples, became a profession—a kind of livelihood! Therefore, Protestant pastors answer the call of Paul, not that of Jesus who defined the qualifications of His disciples as follows:

"If any *man* come to me, and hate not his father, and mother, and wife, and children, and brethren, and sisters, yea, and his own life also, he cannot be my disciple. And whosoever doth not bear his cross, and come after me, cannot be my disciple" (Luke 14:26, 27).

Gospel was given to all. It was not a monopoly of any one. Paul with his limited knowledge of the Gospel wanted to push that amongst the ignorant. This can be seen by the way he was claiming that it was 'his gospel' instead of saying that it was 'their gospel'! That is what we see at several places:

Romans 2

16 In the day when God shall judge the secrets of men by Jesus Christ according to my gospel.

Romans 16

25 Now to him that is of power to stablish you according to my gospel, and the preaching of Jesus Christ, according to the revelation of the mystery, which was kept secret since the world began.

2 Timothy 2

8 Remember that Jesus Christ of the seed of David was raised from the dead according to my gospel.

The question is whether his gospel will lead us to salvation? It cannot be when that contains preaching other than what Jesus did! With lack of communication and distances involved in those times, no wonder Paul went unchecked with his own techniques and theories to win gullible Gentiles by bending the law of Christ to suit their whims and fancies by shelling out compromise formulas pleasing everybody! His argumentative approach in his letters was soothing to carnal minded people! His letters look very much pale in contrast to the dazzling and authoritative words of Jesus in the books of the Gospel. After the Gospel, the books following it are like appendix. Too much use of that has led to appendicitis in Protestants!

Ritual minded Paul did not try to stop an erroneous practice of baptizing for the dead. Instead used it to defend his virtual spirituality in arguments as can be seen from this verse:" Else what shall they do which are baptized for the dead, if the dead rise not at all? Why are they then baptized for the dead?" (1 Corinthians 15:29). This is a glaring example of his shallow understanding of the spiritual standards set by Jesus! Probably, Paul has forgotten that we have the living God, not of the dead!

There are two things that Paul wrote that are likely to encourage indirectly the younger generation when misinterpreted to rebel against parents. The related verses are:

"And, ye fathers, provoke not your children to wrath: but bring them up in the nurture and admonition of the Lord" (Ephesians 6:4), and fathers, provoke not your children to anger, lest they be discouraged" (Colossians 3:21).

So it is easy for younger generation to pick on parents for any advice they may give them as something provoking and against their carnal desires and activities based on the verses mentioned above. God held that children should honour parents. And it was incorporated in the Ten Commandments. Jesus also indicated that no earthly father will think of harming his children, rather he will benefit his children: "If he ask a fish, will he give him a serpent?" (Matthew 7:10).

Generally, though there are bound to be exceptions to this, it is the children who will avoid helping parents in their old age. This was pointed out by Jesus: "For God commanded, saying, Honour thy father and mother: and, He that curseth father or mother, let him die the death. But ye say, Whosoever shall say to *his* father or *his* mother, *It is* a gift, by whatsoever thou mightest be profited by me; And honour not his father or his mother, *he shall be free.* Thus have ye made the commandment of God of none effect by your tradition" (Matthew 15:4 to 6).

But, what is more, Paul even goes to the extent of burdening the parents from what we can see from the following verse:

"Behold, the third time I am ready to come to you; and I will not be burdensome to you: for I seek not yours, but you: for the children ought not to lay up for the parents, but the parents for the children" (2 Corinthians 12:14).

Again this contradicts the preaching of Jesus as not to lay up treasures on earth: Matthew 6:19! How ignorant Paul could be?

No wonder irresponsible younger generation will be demanding too many things to meet their worldly desires as if it is their right to expect from parents!

It is said that Paul is to Christianity what Joseph Smith is to Mormonism—a cult! Paul's spirit is the spirit of anti-Christ though in milder form!

It may be worthwhile to consider the following verses from the OT:

(Deuteronomy 13:1 to 3): "If there arise among you a prophet, or a dreamer of dreams, and giveth thee a sign or a wonder, And the sign or the wonder come to pass, whereof he spake unto thee, saying, Let us go after other gods, which thou hast not known, and let us serve them; Thou shalt not hearken unto the words of that prophet, or that dreamer of dreams: for the LORD your God proveth you, to know whether ye love the LORD your God with all your heart and with all your soul."

More or less this is what we find in Paul's testimony. Instead of telling people to serve other gods, he suggested to imitate him diverting our attention on Jesus. This was noticed by many resulting in rejection of him, and Paul also admitted that in 2 Timothy 1:15: "This thou knowest, that all they which are in Asia be turned away from me; of whom are Phygellus and Hermogenes."

It becomes difficult to understand whether he really got converted to the way of Christ or remained a Pharisee bent upon thrusting his own half-learnt gospel on to people with his compromise formulas to garner support and gain leadership with new believers! Here is another verse that proves my point:

"For we are the circumcision, which worship God in the spirit, and rejoice in Christ Jesus, and have no confidence in the flesh. Though I might also have confidence in the flesh. If any other man thinketh that he hath whereof he might trust in the flesh, I more: circumcised the eighth day, of the stock of Israel, *of* the tribe of Benjamin, an Hebrew of the Hebrews; as touching the law, a Pharisee; concerning zeal, persecuting the church; touching the righteousness which is in the law, blameless" (Philippians 3:3 to 6).

Why was Paul using 'present tense' here in his statements? Had he forgotten that he had become a believer in Jesus? Or, as observed earlier, was he using different trump cards under different situations to derive maximum advantage to peddle his speculations?

Paul appeared to feel greatly—not guilty—by telling lies. This he has confessed in Romans 3:7—'for if the truth of God hath more abounded through my lie unto his glory; why yet am I also judged as a sinner?' This verse can be easily misunderstood by immature believers and evangelists, and they may go out in full swing to make a habit of lying in promoting their version of the truth thereby sacrificing their integrity for their living!

This thinking of his was further endorsed by saying that all kinds of unworthy means can be employed to meet the end of his motive to reach out with his gospel by hook or by crook methods (God forbid such unrighteous desires!): "some indeed preach Christ even of envy and strife; and some also of good will: the one preach Christ of contention, not sincerely, supposing to add affliction to my bonds: but the other of love, knowing that I am set for the defence of the gospel. What then? Notwithstanding, every way, whether in pretence, or in truth, Christ is preached; and I therein do rejoice, yea, and will rejoice" (Philippians 1:15 to 18).

The means employed should justify the mission for all believers in the truth of Jesus Christ.

Let us consider another verse: "Christ hath redeemed us from the curse of the law, being made a curse for us: for it is written, Cursed is every one that hangeth on a tree" (Galatians 3:13).

The Law was not meant to curse us; instead it was meant to escape from the wrath of God when transgressed! Law is not a curse. We have from Psalm 19:8: "The statutes of the LORD are right, rejoicing the heart: the commandment of the LORD is pure, enlightening the eyes."

We have comments of well known personalities that are indicated below against their names. I think they are all authenticated statements. I have already indicated what Mahatma Gandhi opinionated about Paul's work in my introduction at the beginning.

"Paul's words are not the Words of God. They are the words of Paul- a vast difference." (Thomas Jefferson).

"Paul was the first corrupter of the doctrines of Jesus." (Carl Sagan (Scientist; Author))

"My long-time view about Christianity is that it represents an amalgam of two seemingly immiscible parts--the religion of Jesus and the religion of Paul. Thomas Jefferson attempted to excise the Pauline parts of the New Testament. There wasn't much left when he was done, but it was an inspiring document." (Letter to Ken Schei [author of Christianity Betrayed])(Albert Schweitzer)

"Where possible Paul avoids quoting the teaching of Jesus, in fact even mentioning it. If we had to rely on Paul, we should not know that Jesus taught in parables, had delivered the sermon on the mount, and had taught His disciples the 'Our Father.' Even where they are specially relevant, Paul passes over the words of the Lord."(Wil Durant (Philosopher)).

"Paul created a theology of which none but the vaguest warrants can be found in the words of Christ. Fundamentalism is the triumph of Paul over Christ"(Walter Kaufmann (Professor of Philosophy, Princeton)).

"Paul substituted faith in Christ for the Christ like life" (George Bernard Shaw).

"No sooner had Jesus knocked over the dragon of superstition than Paul boldly set it on its legs again in the name of Jesus" (Thomas Hardy).

"The new testament was less a Christiad than a Pauliad."(Hyam Maccoby (Talmudic Scholar))

"As we have seen, the purposes of the book of Acts are to minimize the conflict between Paul and the leaders of the Jerusalem Church, James and Peter. Peter and Paul, in later Christian tradition, became twin saints, brothers in faith, and the idea that they were historically bitter opponents standing for irreconcilable religious standpoints would have been repudiated with horror. The work of the author of Acts was well done; he rescued Christianity from the imputation of being the individual creation of Paul, and instead gave it a respectable pedigree, as a doctrine with the authority of the so-called Jerusalem Church, conceived as continuous in spirit with the Pauline Gentile Church of Rome. Yet, for all his efforts, the truth of the matter is not hard to recover, if we examine the New Testament evidence with an eye to tell-tale inconsistencies and confusions, rather than with the determination to gloss over and harmonize all difficulties in the interests of an orthodox interpretation." (The Mythmaker, p.139,Weidenfeld and Nicolson, London, 1986) (Jeremy Bentham (English Philosopher).

"If Christianity needed an Anti-Christ, they needed look no farther than Paul." (Paraphrased. Looking for a copy of "Not Paul, but Jesus" in order to retrieve the exact quote.)

It's obvious that Paul's teachings are not in agreement with the teachings of Jesus, so therefore, it is deception camouflaged at best! Sorry to say but in many cases Christians quote a lot of Paul's writings so in actuality they follow the teachings of Paul not God's or Jesus'. Of course, Catholic clergy and saints and other true believers of Christ do not resort to that. They only quote Paul if that harmonizes with what Jesus preached. That is my stand too!

The ego centric Paul wrote treating the chosen semi-literate apostles as not worthy of consideration putting them in poor light and seeking limelight on him!

First, Paul did not listen to the twelve apostles. Paul rails in Galatians 2:1-9 at the three "so-called" apostolic pillars of the Jerusalem church (*words used are 'seemed to be'*) (including John) (Gal. 2:9). Paul says again they were "reputed to be something" (Gal. 2:2, 6), but "whatsoever they were it makes no difference to me; God does not accept a man's person [i.e., judge by their position and rank]." (Gal. 2:6.) Paul then expressly declares that he received nothing from the twelve apostles.

I say [those] who were of repute [i.e., the apostles in context] *imparted nothing to me*, but contrariwise they saw that I was entrusted with the gospel of the uncircumcision. (Gal. 2:7.)

Paul was boasting of his failure to take any information about Jesus' teachings from the original apostles at Jerusalem. He claimed his failure to do so was positive proof his message for Gentiles came direct from God. Paul puts a spin on his behaviour that he would be a lesser figure in Christendom had he learned anything about Jesus from the twelve!

Please read all the commentaries you can on those verses. They all agree on this characterization of Paul's meaning. Read the verses yourself to verify the disdain Paul was expressing toward learning anything about Jesus from the apostles or the reputed pillars of the church–Peter, John, and James.

Now listen again to what John–one of the three mentioned by Paul as "seeming pillars"–had to say about this kind of behavior. John writes:

We belong to God, and everyone who knows God will listen to us [*i.e.*, the twelve apostles]. But the people who don't know God won't listen to us. That is how we can tell the Spirit that speaks the truth from the one that tells lies. (1 John 4:6)

John clearly would regard someone such as Paul who refused to learn from the twelve as someone who does not "know God." The fact Paul would not listen to the twelve (and was proud of it) allows us to realize Paul is one who "tells lies," if we accept John's direction.

Next, we shall consider another question: Did Papias understand John's epistle message was against Paul?

The only later figure whom we confidently can conclude knew Apostle John is Papias. He was John's pupil. Papias appears to have understood Apostle John was criticizing Paul. The surviving fragments of the writings of Papias, bishop of Hierapolis (130 A.D.) "do not contain any quotation from Paul" even while quoting John's Gospel and 1 Peter. 4 This and other evidence led Christian scholar Charles M. Nielsen to argue that Papias was writing "against a growing `Paulinis' [*i.e.*, Paulinism] in Asia Minor circa 125-135 A.D., just prior to full blown Marcionism [*i.e.*, Paul-only-ism]." 5 Nielsen contends Papias' opponent was Polycarp, bishop of Smyrna, who favored Paul. (We have more to say on Polycarp in a moment.)

Thus, in Papias–a bishop of the early church and close associate of Apostle John–we find a figure who already is fighting a growing Paulinism in pre-Marcion times. This allows an inference that Apostle John shared the same concern about Paul that we identify in John's letters. Apostle John then passed on his concern to Papias. This led Papias to fight the "growing Paulinis" (*i.e.*, Paulinism) in Asia Minor–the region to which Ephesus belonged.

Paul's view of himself as an apostle didn't stop at just claiming to be an apostle. He did what he could to communicate to his followers that he was the biggest and the best. He even had the nerve to challenge the very apostles Jesus had called and trained for over three years! Among the many self-admiring quotes are these:

"For I suppose I was not a whit behind the very chiefest apostles" and "and as the truth of Christ is in me, no man shall stop me of this boasting in the regions of Achaia" (2 Corinthians 5, 10).

Sometimes, almost as though he knew he should be ashamed of such claims, he would tie his claim to a statement of unworthiness. Apparently he thought the gullible would embrace him as the greatest of apostles because he was so humble.

"For I am the least of the apostles, that am not meet to be called an apostle, because I persecuted the church of God. But by the grace of God I am what I am: and his grace *which was bestowed* upon me was not in vain; but I laboured more abundantly than they all: yet not I, but the grace of God which was with me. (1 Corinthians 15:9,10)

To the Galatians, Paul makes no pretense about how he compares himself to Peter, James, and John:

"But of these who seemed to be somewhat, (whatsoever they were, it maketh no matter to me: God accepteth no man's person:) for they who seemed *to be somewhat* in conference added nothing to me: But contrariwise, when they saw that the gospel of the uncircumcision was committed unto me, as *the gospel* of the circumcision *was* unto Peter........And when James, Cephas, and John, who seemed to be pillars, perceived the grace that was given unto me, they gave to me and Barnabas the right hands of fellowship; that we *should go* unto the heathen, and they unto the circumcision" (Galatians 2:6, 7 & 9).

Then Paul goes on to describe how hypocritical Peter was being for living a different gospel from the one that he (Paul) preached. It is interesting to note that earlier in the book (Galatians. 1:8, 9) Paul commanded his followers to damn, (curse, or doom to destruction), anyone who preaches a different gospel than that which he had preached. According to him then, that would include damning Peter, if not James and John also! It is obvious to the reader of the first two chapters of Galatians, that Paul was demanding that the Galatian church follow no one but him, not even the original apostles back in Jerusalem.

As a side note it should also be noted that Paul himself was being the real hypocrite when he condemned Peter for accommodating Gentiles when he was around Gentiles and acting like a Jew around Jews because in another place Paul said:

"For though I be free from all *men,* yet have I made myself servant unto all, that I might gain the more. And unto the Jews I became as a Jew, that I might gain the Jews; to them that are under the law, as under the law, that I might gain them that are under the law; to them that are without law, as without law, (being not without law to God, but under the law to Christ,) that I might gain them that are without law. To the weak became I as weak, that I might gain the weak: I am made all things to all *men,* that I might by all means save some" (1 Corinthians 9:19-22).

A little later in the same letter Paul said:

"Whether therefore ye eat, or drink, or whatsoever ye do, do all to the glory of God. Give none offence, neither to the Jews, nor to the Gentiles, nor to the church of God:even as I please all *men* in all *things,* not seeking mine own profit, but the *profit* of many, that they may be saved" (1 Corinthians 10:31-33).

So here we have Paul claiming to be greater than any other apostle. He insulted Peter, James, and John by saying they only *"seemed"* to be pillars of the church and they were nothing to him. He bragged about how he told off Peter, and he subtly curses the apostles by telling the Galatians to consider accursed anyone who differs with him. All this, while in fact, *he* was being the greatest hypocrite of all! If anyone else had even begun to do and say the things that Paul did we would have recognized their incredible conceit and rejected them a long time ago. Solomon said it well,

"Boast not thyself of tomorrow; for thou knowest not what a day may bring forth. Let another man praise thee, and not thine own mouth; a stranger, and not thine own lips" (Proverbs 27:2)

8

Some Scholarly Studies on the Saint

This is what Albert Schweitzer wrote in his book, "*The Quest for the Historical Jesus*":

"The attitude which Paul himself takes up towards the Gospel of Jesus is that he does not repeat it in the words of Jesus, and does not appeal to its authority.... The fateful thing is that the Greek, the Catholic, and the Protestant theologies all contain the Gospel of Paul in a form which does not continue the Gospel of Jesus, but displaces it."

We have additional reviews:

(a) The Pauline "Christians" that exist today do not follow Christ, they should be called Paulians. The true Christians were the Nazarenes and Ebionites that no longer exist.

(b) "Paul deviated people towards lawlessness, through his strange philosophy that, the observance of the Law motivates to sin, thus justifying his innovation regarding the abolition of the Law!"

(c) There is so much diversity and clash, so much chaos, in the Christian Church today that the old idea of a unified or systematic Christian truth has gone. For this, the ecumenical movement is too late. What has happened is that the Christian world has moved into that situation of open variety, of optional alternatives. It would seem no longer possible for anyone to be told or even to imagine that he can be told, what it means or should mean, formally and generically, to be a Christian. He must decide for himself and only for himself *(Christianity on Trial, I, Colin Chapman, pp. 51-52)*

(d) The point comes home best when one considers Paul's explicit statement that the human individual can do nothing himself to secure salvation, "(cf. Rom. 3,24; 3,28; 9,11; 9,16; 1.Cor. 1,29; Gal. 2,16). For according to Paul salvation depends solely on the Grace of God" (Eph. 2, 8-9).

Thus the Pauline doctrine makes salvation a one-sided matter for God; people on earth have their hands bound (cf. Rom. 3, 24; 4, 16; Eph. 2, 5; 2, 8-9; 2 Tim. 1, 9; Tit. 3, 5-7). What Paul says here is of course quite attractive, because it is comfortable. By joining the fold, salvation ensues "automatically". No effort on one's own part is then necessary to arrive at the goal of life, for every Christian is saved once and for all by the sacrificial death of Jesus on the cross at Golgotha.

It means that one has only to sign up with this "institution", pay the "membership fee", and (lo and behold!) everything is settled for securing a seat in paradise for all eternity. Naturally such a teaching attracted many supporters and spread rapidly. After all it is easier to believe in something that can be had safely and comfortably!

Simply by the simple act of conversion a person is then redeemed, saved, made a child of God, and becomes a completely new person. According to this teaching, every attempt on one's own part to work towards salvation plays down Jesus' role, is even a deadly sin. And conversely, every person, however exemplary and good his or her life may have been, is declared by his teaching to be lost if he or she does not gratefully acknowledge the sacrifice of the cross as constituting their entire personal salvation.

Most Christians think the greatness and uniqueness of Christianity stands and falls with the truth of his [Paul's] teaching. On closer inspection, however, it is found to be a fabrication, far removed from the real ideas of Jesus. There is no hint of the so called Christian doctrine of salvation in the gospels, either in the Sermon on the Mount - the quintessence of Jesus' message - or in the Our Father, or the traditional parables of Jesus!

Jesus did not supply theories to be ground in the mills of academia, about his path and message -- he just lived his teaching!

(e) The following two excerpts from an earlier book, "The Dead Sea Scrolls Deception" also raise doubts as to the legitimacy of Paul's role within the early church:(by Michael Bajgent and Richard Leigh (Corgi Books, London, 1991))

"... Paul is in effect the first Christian heretic, and his teachings, which become the foundation of later Christianity, are a flagrant deviation from the 'Original' or 'pure' form extolled by the leadership. Whether James, the 'Lord's brother,' was literally Jesus' blood kin or not (and everything suggests he was), it is clear that he knew Jesus...personally. So did most of the other members of the community or 'early Church,' in Jerusalem, including of course, Peter. When they spoke, they did so with first hand authority. Paul had never had such personal acquaintance with the figure he'd begun to regard as his 'Saviour.' He had only his quasi-mystical experience in the desert and the sound of a disembodied voice. For him to arrogate authority to himself on this basis is, to say the least, presumptuous. It also leads him to distort Jesus' teachings beyond recognition, to formulate, in fact, his own highly individual and idiosyncratic theology, and then to legitimise it by spuriously ascribing it to Jesus."

"As things transpired, however, the mainstream of the new movement gradually coalesced, during the next three centuries, around Paul and his teachings. Thus, to the undoubted posthumous horror of James and his associates, an entirely new religion was indeed born, a religion that came to have less and less to do with its supposed founder."

(f) "The Spirit of the Apostles is not a guide equal or greater than the Lord, thus Paul within his letters does not have as much authority as has Christ." (Carlstadt, Canonicis Scripturis (1520)

(g) "In the teachings of Christ, religion is completely present tense: Jesus is the prototype and our task is to imitate him, become a disciple. But then through Paul came a basic alteration. Paul draws attention away from imitating Christ and fixes attention on the death of Christ the Atoner. What Martin Luther, in his reformation, failed to realize is that even before Catholicism, Christianity had become degenerate at the hands of Paul. Paul made Christianity the religion of Paul, not of Christ Paul threw the Christianity of Christ away, completely turning it upside down. Making it just the opposite of the original proclamation of Christ" (Soren Kierkegaard, Theologian)

(h) "True Christianity, which will last forever, comes from the gospel words of Christ not from the epistles of Paul. The writings of Paul have been a danger and a hidden rock. The cause of the principal defects of Christian theology." (Theologian Ernest Renan, Saint Paul[/i])

(i) "The Marcionists (a Christian sect) assumed that the evangelists were filled with falsities. The Manicheans, who formed a very large sect at the commencement of Christianity, rejected as false all the New Testament, and showed other writings quite different that they gave for authentic. The Cerinthians, like the Marcionists, admitted not the Acts of the Apostles. The Encratites, and the Sévénians, adopted neither the Acts nor the Epistles of Paul. Chrysostom, in a homily which he made upon the Acts of the Apostles, says that in his time, about the year 400, many people knew nothing either of the author or of the book. St. Irene, who lived before that time, reports that the Valentinians, like several other sects of Christians, accused the Scriptures of being filled with imperfections, errors and contradictions. The Ebionites, or Nazarenes, who were the first Christians, rejected all the Epistles of Paul and regarded him as an impostor. They report, among other things, that he was originally a pagan, that he came to Jerusalem, where he lived some time; and that having a mind to marry the daughter of the high priest, he caused himself to be circumcised; but that not being able to obtain her, he quarreled with the Jews and wrote against circumcision, and against the observance of the Sabbath, and against all the legal ordinances. – (Boulanger-Critical examination of Paul).

(j) At the start of Christianity stand two figures: Jesus and Paul. Jesus is regarded by Christians as the founder of their religion, the events of his life comprise the foundation story of Christianity; but Paul is regarded as the great interpreter of Jesus' mission, who explained, in a way that Jesus himself never did, how Jesus' life and death fitted into a universal scheme of salvation, stretching from the creation of Adam to the end of time.

How do we understand the relationship between Jesus and Paul? What would Jesus himself have thought of Paul? We know that Jesus never knew Paul; the two men never once met. How did the disciples who knew Jesus best, such as Peter, James and John view Paul? Did they agree with the interpretations disseminated by Paul in his fluent, articulate writings? Or did they perhaps think that this newcomer to the scene, spinning complicated theories about the place of Jesus in the scheme of things, was getting everything wrong?

Paul claimed that his interpretations were not just his own invention, but had come to him by personal inspiration; he claimed that he had personal acquaintance with the resurrected Jesus, even though he had never met him during his lifetime. Incredibly he claimed that such acquaintance, gained through visions and transports, was actually superior to acquaintance with Jesus during his lifetime, when (according to Paul) Jesus was much more reticent about his purposes.

9

Some Appropriate Verses of Paul

In spite of the tirade against Paul, I do acknowledge a few verses of his that are encouraging for spiritual life since they compliment the preaching of Jesus. Here are some of them:

2 Corinthians 12

9 And he said unto me, My grace is sufficient for thee: for my strength is made perfect in weakness. Most gladly therefore will I rather glory in my infirmities, that the power of Christ may rest upon me.

Colossians 3:

1 If ye then be risen with Christ, seek those things which are above, where Christ sitteth on the right hand of God.

2 Set your affection on things above, not on things on the earth.

1 Corinthians 9:27 But I keep under my body, and bring *it* into subjection: lest that by any means, when I have preached to others, I myself should be a castaway.

Philippians 2

12 Wherefore, my beloved, as ye have always obeyed, not as in my presence only, but now much more in my absence, work out your own salvation with fear and trembling.

Romans 8

[1] There is therefore now no condemnation to them which are in Christ Jesus, who walk not after the flesh, but after the Spirit.

1 Corinthians 6

[19] Or do you not know that your body is a temple of the Holy Spirit who is in you, whom you have from God, and that you are not your own?

Galatians 5:

[22] But the fruit of the Spirit is love, joy, peace, longsuffering, gentleness, goodness, faith,

[23] Meekness, temperance:

Galatians 6

[10] So then, while we have opportunity, let us do good to all people, and especially to those who are of the household of the faith.

Conclusion

For an honest seeker of truth, it is very clear that Paul was semi-anti-Christ and anti-apostles right from the very beginning of his ministry in association with Jerusalem Church. His writings are not even a shadow of the preaching of Jesus who decides our salvation. In contrast it is not the case with other writings in the NT.

Those who are dead spiritually, naturally, flow with the current like a dead fish! Opportunists and hypocrites are interpreting conveniently for an easy life sans sacrifice, sharing, suffering, and serving. It is just virtual spirituality to the masses with abundant supply of salvation packages of all kinds. I am concerned because of these verses of Peter:

"But the day of the Lord will come as a thief in the night; in the which the heavens shall pass away with a great noise, and the elements shall melt with fervent heat, the earth also and the works that are therein shall be burned up. *Seeing* then *that* all these things shall be dissolved, what manner *of persons* ought ye to be in *all* holy conversation and godliness, looking for and hasting unto the coming of the day of God, wherein the heavens being on fire shall be dissolved, and the elements shall melt with fervent heat? Nevertheless we, according to his promise, look for new heavens and a new earth, wherein dwelleth righteousness. Wherefore, beloved, seeing that ye look for such things, be diligent that ye may be found of him in peace, without spot, and blameless.

And account *that* the longsuffering of our Lord *is* salvation; even as our beloved brother Paul also according to the wisdom given unto him hath written unto you; as also in all *his* epistles, speaking in them of these things; in which are some things hard to be understood, which they that are unlearned and unstable wrest, as *they do* also the other scriptures, unto their own destruction.

Ye therefore, beloved, seeing ye know *these things* before, beware lest ye also, being led away with the error of the wicked, fall from your own stedfastness. But grow in grace, and *in* the knowledge of our Lord and Saviour Jesus Christ. To him *be* glory both now and forever. Amen" (2 Peter 3:10-18).

Many scholars think that the second epistle of Peter is forged. How much Marcion altered or added to this, we do not know. Ignoring such a charge, one can see that the chief apostle, Peter, calling Paul as his beloved brother in an exemplary Christian manner despite his opposition to him. I am sure even Peter with his limited scholarly background would have found Paul's unnecessary expositions based on his wisdom (not that of the Holy Spirit) hard to understand!

Again, as a true apostle in charge of rendering service to the flock, warns of self-inflicted destruction of many because of misinterpretations and ear tickling theories that go with Paul's epistles in general.

Therefore, it is high time that we read and study the books of the Gospel with prayer and devotion. In this endeavour the Gospel according to John, the beloved of Jesus, should be given highest importance because of its spiritual approach followed by Matthew, Mark and Luke in that order.

May the Prince of peace bless you in knowing the truth to walk in the way that leads to eternal life! Amen.